MY CHARLES STREET

A MEMOIR

BY

ANNA STROSSER

My Charles Street

ISBN 978-0-9823766-2-1

Library of Congress Control Number: 2009913339

Editor
Margie Strosser

Cover Design
Bette Waters

Cover Painting
Anna Strosser

McDonough Press
1619 S. 13th Street
Philadelphia, PA 19148

For my mother and father,
Bridget McDonough Berry and John Berry

ANNA BERRY STROSSER
AT AGE 16

Acknowledgement

I owe a great deal of credit for this memoir to poet Patricia Dobler, teacher of the Mad Women of the Attic program at the Women's Creative Writing Center, Carlow College in Pittsburgh, for getting me started on this journey. I wish to thank my daughter, Margie Strosser, for her help and patience, and for her invaluable job of editing.

Anna Strosser
Philadelphia, 2009

TABLE OF CONTENTS

PROLOGUE

Every story is about an event or number of events. No one's life can be tracked fully every minute of every day and that is where life is, in the minutes of each day. They pile up on each other. Some drop out when new ones arrive, some are so dense with emotion that they cling and become the path of life. The moments that I remember are the ones that had that quality of staying at the top of the heap. Sometimes the sad ones or the demeaning ones or the frightening ones leap over the happy ones and overcome them, so that the happy ones are forgotten. Then a whole period of time can be completely overshadowed by bad memories and it's a struggle to dig down and find the happy or pleasant ones that must have been there. The sad and frightening ones on Charles Street are well known to me; so I need to probe my mind and find the light filled ones, like a large window that fills some parts of a room with light and leaves the rest in shadow. My sister Betty loved that house and that neighborhood, so my unhappiness with it had to have been in my thinking.

I hated our house! It seemed so dark and dreary. Maybe I just felt that way because Daddy was drunk so much of the time, Mama was always mad at something or out working scrubbing floors at Montefiore Hospital. We were not allowed to talk to the neighbors because we might tell them something about my father. We weren't allowed to play with the other children on the street. I guess the rules were to keep us safe. To Mama it was a dangerous world, a different danger than the ones in Ireland. Not that I know what the dangers were there, but she lived in a little cottage on an island, surrounded by sea on all sides. Maybe things happened to children over there, maybe they would fall in the ocean and drown if they didn't stay in the house all the time.

I would think that the six of us being by ourselves so much of the time would make us partners or friends. But no, I

9

think it made us more separate. I spent a lot of time by myself, reading, doing housework, watching the others. I wondered if they watched me. We all went our own way to home from school, or church. Sometimes it seems like a movie. I can see their faces and their clothes, but never know what they are thinking about anything.

We did what we were told to do, afraid of something that might happen if we didn't, going to hell or, even worse, having Mama mad at us. Her anger was fierce; she put her hands on her hips, brought her mouth down as far as it would go, stared at us with those blue, blue eyes, whipped out a spoon or raised her hand and we did as she said because we didn't want that hand or spoon stinging our bottoms. But her love was fierce, too, and that was what we all wanted, I guess. She was the only one in the family that I knew. She didn't say much, but I understood her actions. She held me gently when I was sick, she cooked oatmeal at night so it would be creamy in the morning, she went to the welfare to get food and clothes, ugly ones most of the time, for us. She was even nice to Daddy when he was working and not drinking.

I watched the neighborhood, too. They were all so mysterious. I imagined what their houses were like, how their families lived.

I always thought I wanted to tell stories because my father was fond of storytelling. But my mother was the one who loved to listen, and read stories. She loved the story in the daily paper. I read it too, trying to see what was so important about saving it for her. She went to the movies, and no matter how broke we were she found the few pennies extra so I could go with her. We saw every movie that we could during the Thirties and early Nineteen Forties. And we never talked about them. Her enjoyment seemed quiet, wordless. Her words were more often connected to anger. How easily the mind gets boxed in. I had to get behind the anger to find the love, a difficult task that is always a process.

I still love stories. I think that stories were all my parents had. It's easier to tell a story than to write one, maybe because it's easier to lie with words that are less permanent; they aren't written down. The telling is less fearful in a repressed, outlawed society such as the west of Ireland was when my parents were growing up. The stories that I heard came out of the sea and the rocky land, from the need to keep secrets from the English who had held them in bondage for centuries, from the Guarda, the Irish police, who apparently carried on the tradition; and from the Catholic priests who made sure of it. Stories of scratching a living from seaweed and rocks, of making poteen, the home made liquor distilled from the barley that would grow between those rocks.

I listened to the soft Irish brogues at gatherings of Daddy's brothers, their tongues loosened by whiskey, at the wakes where the life of the dead was re-told in full and glorious detail; and in the sober conversations among the women working in the kitchen. I never dared to interrupt by asking questions or I would never hear the end of the particular story being told. Not that it mattered. Irish stories didn't end, they were left dangling with an exclamation of dismay or sadness or with laughter all around, obscuring the meaning of the tale. Maybe because life was hard so much of the time in Ireland the stories were cover ups, grim humor made up out of grief, the only way to make life bearable. It's easier for the survivors to live with the heroic memories than the tragic ones.

I realized in some way that many of these stories could not be true, but trying to understand the difference between stories and lies was confusing. Sometimes the story was explained by calling it a "little white lie." I could not figure out why the white lies were more acceptable than regular lies, which were not called "big black lies." But then I never could figure out a lot of things, because I never asked. And no one ever asked me what I thought about this world that was new to my parents, familiar but confusing to me. Eons later I found out that making sense of the world is a lost cause. Maybe that's why people become dependent on religion like my family was;

somebody assures you that it will all come out right in the end.

So this story is a search for the truth that lies tell. I thought I had a miserable life as a child, that we lived in a dark house (row houses do tend to be dark), in a hostile neighborhood, that our mother disciplined us too much or that she and my father ignored us. The search leads me to things that I didn't know about myself; that only came alive when I looked at the words I had written down. The written word changed the story; it became light and clear. The anger and the envy and the sadness drifted in and out but the light revealed some of the everyday loving and happy things. It helped me to live with memories, not tragic but often sad and sometimes joyful, and put them in a perspective that allows the good ones to rise to the top of my mind. Like the Irish stories, this story of my life on Charles Street goes roundabout and stops at various other bits of stories; and the long reach of it is comforting in my old age.

Fragments of Life

Fragments of my life float
like pieces of a puzzle
in the muck and the rain
none of them fitting together
edges curled, colors dim
or brilliant.

Maybe I could do
what they do when restoring old films
fix the colors, straighten the edges
brighten the background
integrate the pieces.

Seizures

The seizure is a sudden alteration of behavior or consciousness caused by abnormal electrical activity in the brain. Seizures come in many forms; some involve convulsive activity such as jerking movements or stiffening of the body; others are exhibited by simply staring off into space.

The most common seizure typically begins with sudden changes in level of alertness, followed by shaking or stiffening of the body lasting several minutes. Often these seizures are followed by a period of sleepiness, and may include temporary paralysis that can last anywhere from minutes to hours. While first time seizures that last less than three to five minutes may be frightening, most are not serious.

Breath-holding spells may be confused with seizure disorder and are associated with loss of consciousness, and changes in postural tone. These spells are most common in children between six and eighteen months and usually disappear after five years of age.

Breath-holding in young children is usually

precipitated by anger or frustration although it may also occur after a painful experience.

CHAPTER ONE

The House

Two galvanized metal washtubs were on the kitchen floor, one filled with cold water, the other with hot or maybe warm water. I was hiding under the kitchen table. Some of the water dripped on the red and cream colored octagon shaped tile, making the red tiles darker and making clear drops on the cream ones. Mama was bent over the tub, her head down, so I could see only the bush of hair, the fine lines of the hairnet that kept it from springing out. She had a towel, white, over her right shoulder, her sleeves were rolled up high on her arms. She was holding my sister Betty, who must have been one or maybe two years old. Betty was shaking so hard that Mama was holding her very tight. Dr. Wallace, a mild, older man with sparks of white above his ears, was kneeling on one knee at the side of the other tub.

"Gently, now, Bridget," Dr. Wallace said. Without answering, Mama carefully lowered Betty into the water, holding her head above water level.

"All right, now give her to me," he said. Holding her firmly he lowered her into the other tub,

They quickly moved the baby from one tub to the other for some minutes. There was no sound until Betty started crying and then they stopped. Mama wrapped her in the towel and sat in front of the oven holding her while Dr. Wallace emptied the water from the tubs. Then he sat down beside her and talked to her for a while.

Mama told me much later that Betty had convulsions and that this was the standard method of treatment, moving the baby from cold water to hot water until the seizures stopped. For the rest of us, the seizures gave Betty a privileged place in the family. She was very high strung and we were forbidden to aggravate her in any way that might have brought them on again. We did tease her of course, when Mama wasn't around to stop us. It was hard not to argue with Betty because she was a very excitable, smart person. And she never had the mysterious seizures again until she was over seventy, when they returned as suddenly as they arrived. To me, it was a medical puzzle, somewhat like the return of polio to some people who had it in their childhood.

Mama said I was too young to remember, but the picture of the treatment for seizures is so real in my mind that it's hard for me to believe that I wasn't there. I wonder if a person can really remember something that happened when they were very young, or if the memory comes from forming a picture in your mind when somebody is telling about an incident and it becomes your own story?

At that time babies were born at home, although some must have been born in hospitals. We had six children in our family, all of us born at home. When Joe, the youngest, was born, Dr. Wallace came to our house sometime during the night. My sister Mary and I stood in the bedroom doorway the following morning, speechless. This time I know I was there. Daddy was standing by the partially shuttered window, his black hair and dark clothes blending into the dim light of the room. His presence was eclipsed by the presence of the doctor, and the baby. I hardly noticed him, I was so entranced by the appearance of Joe. Daddy was still around then, not like later, when he was gone much of the time.

Mama was lying in the big bed; the dark headboard was curved inward at both ends. Dr. Wallace leaned on the footboard. It seemed odd to me that he was standing beside the bed, looking at Mama and talking about the baby. He smiled at us, giving us tiny, sweet pink pills, "baby pills," he called them. The dark wood shutters were closed over the bottom part of the windows but the top shutters were open and Mama smiled at us, a rare treat.

A visiting nurse came every day for a while, carrying her black leather case that looked like my mother's big purse. She wore a grey dress and a small grey hat on the side of her head; her black shoes were like my mother's, too, sturdy and sensible. She didn't give out candy but she was skillful and nice and smiled at us. She came once or twice a week for a few weeks and often fixed lunch for us when she was there.

I remember Dr. Wallace and that unnamed nurse as loving examples. They were kind and competent and treated us with respect, something which we did not always get when we went to the welfare to get clothes and food.

Charles Street was long, perhaps a mile or so on the north side of Pittsburgh. But my Charles Street, my world for the length of my childhood, was halfway up one block of that mile, a long series of about forty row houses that were known as party wall houses. My Charles Street was a house bounded by a street, a sidewalk of bricks in chevron pattern, a cement curb. It had a flat, low front step, a higher top step good for sitting, and double doors to lean against. Beyond the doors, one of which was kept open, was the marble floor of the vestibule, or maybe it was little white ceramic tiles, good for sitting in behind the closed door when it was hot and sunny outside and I needed a place to read.

The vestibule doors were of wood, no glass. The large door leading into the hall had cut glass in the top part. When the outside doors were open and the sun was allowed to sneak in, the glass fractured into prisms of pale yellow and lavender with small shafts of light green. The hallway beyond the doors was as large as a small room. On the right as you went in was a low, ornate umbrella stand that had an umbrella holder on each end of a long slab of marble. A mirror, showing patches of black where the silver backing had worn off, stretched almost to the ceiling. There were various fancy carvings of what looked somewhat like flowers and leaves on the base and sides. The telephone, a long, black tube on a curved base with a circle of numbers, and a receiver that clicked when you picked it up from a hook on the side, sat on this monstrous piece of furniture. Daddy used to holler into it sometimes, but I never saw anybody else use it. Maybe it was just a prop left over from the time before the depression when the rich people lived there.

To the left of the hall was a living room. It sometimes had furniture in it, but was probably our parents' bedroom most of the time. The long windows with dark inside shutters were nearly always closed. Between the windows was a long mirror, almost floor to ceiling, with a small marble shelf close to the floor where the mirror ended. Around the top of the walls was a curved and patterned border, a cornice which concealed the jointure between wall and ceiling. It was white and seemed to be of plaster but could have been wood, I suppose. The detailed indications of former wealth were just unexplainable oddities at the time. It never occurred to me that whoever owned that house, and many other houses in the neighborhood, must have hit bad times too.

Next to the living room was the middle room. I don't think of it as the dining room, although I know that there was a large dining room table in there at one time before one of us jumped down from the sideboard and broke it in two. I'm inclined to blame Betty, but that's going back to an old habit. The sideboard was high with small cupboards on the ends, each about a foot or two square. The doors had a nice click when you opened or closed them. The one on the left often had kittens in it. Or maybe only one time. The kittens had a tiny mew and had incredibly soft, dark fur. They didn't last long. My impression is that Daddy put them in a bag and took them down to the river. I can see him going down the dusty road with his giant steps, his head down and a sack in his hand. He never told us and neither did Mama, but Jackie, my older brother, found out and made me sad by telling me.

The kitchen was very large and had two windows that took up most of the back wall. The tops seemed to be near the ceiling and the sill was comfortably placed so that I could lean out without much trouble when I was old enough to take clothes off the pulley line. This was a clothes line that was attached by pulleys to our window sill and to the building at the far end of our back yard. The rope felt rough when you pulled it. Somehow, I feel that it was heavy but I can't actually remember pulling it in when there were clothes on it. Mama boiled clothes, too, white sheets and towels. Bleach was one of those household helps that was unheard of at the time so the dirt and germs had to be boiled out. She had a large, brownish vessel with high sides and a lid. I've seen some since then and they were copper. She used a stick to move the clothes around and to take them out when they had boiled long enough. She shaved pieces of fels-naptha soap and put them in with the clothes. It had a special smell, the flavor of the soap and made the water feel slippery when it was cooled down. There was also a line in the kitchen. This hung from the windows across to one of the doors. Some clothes were hung above the stove; the oven door was often open with clothes lying on it. Mama sometimes sat in front of the oven, her skirt over knees, making a soft surface, holding baby Joe, washing and dressing him. That was a pleasant memory; she was humming or singing, Irish, maybe. The Irish had a cadence, soft as jelly when it was pleasant, harsh as the black rocks of Connemara when it was angry.

The floor had those octagon shaped tiles; each tile was about three inches in diameter. I spent a lot of time looking at that floor, either scrubbing it or sitting on it under the table. The table was a huge, square oak with no center post, so there was lots of room for sitting or playing house. Across from the table was the sink near the window; the stove, a large floor to ceiling cupboard made of light oak, rather yellow and artificial looking. Most of our food was kept there, including bags of dried fruit that we got from the welfare: prunes, apricots, and maybe pears. Next to that was a built-in cupboard that was in two sections. The top had glass doors and we kept dishes in there. There was an extension in front of it and the bottom shelves were deeper, too deep and dark for me to look into. Next to that cupboard was a clothes chute at the bottom of two other shelves. Jack used to slide down to the basement that way. I tried it once and that was enough for me, it was too dark and scary.

The door to the back porch was kept closed most of the time. The ice box was out there but no other furniture so there was lots of room to play in the summertime. The wall between our house and the one next door was brick, and had holes in it, giving us the opportunity to watch the neighbors when Mama wasn't watching us.

There were steep steps leading down to the backyard. They were pretty scary but not as much as going through the cellar to get to the yard. To do that you had to go through the front cellar, a place so dark that even on the brightest day the little windows let in only a crack of light. When I had to go down there I would creep down the steps slowly and when I hit bottom I would race to the light coming from the back part of the cellar. There were no basements then, only cellars.

The first floor was where our life was lived and I thought little about the upper floors where the bedrooms were. Usually the second floor was rented out and we shared the only bathroom with the renters. We children slept on the third floor most of the time and there was nothing in those rooms except our beds.

Going outside was like entering another familiar room. I knew only the outsides of houses, since we rarely went inside any house but our own, and the black asphalt street with a street car track lined with smooth, grey Belgian blocks, strong enough to support the noisy street car clattering its wheels and clanging its bell. I spent a great part of my childhood sitting on the steps of our house on Charles Street. The curbs lining each side of the street made good seats to watch the rain gather into streams and run down toward the corner, or scrape peach stones by the hour to wear them down until a hole appeared that was supposed to become a whistle. I could never do it, but some kids said it was possible. I studied the sidewalks as I tried to avoid lines and cracks, thinking of the rhyme that stepping on cracks would break your mother's back. But it was impossible to avoid the lines because the patterns of the bricks changed in front of each series of houses. I know it was a superstition, but I was afraid that if I stepped on one it might give my mother more backaches than she had already.

I watched the people on our block. I can still remember what they looked like and about some parts of their lives that were lived on the small cement porches, the sidewalks and on the street.

We all agree, when I talk to my sisters now, seventy years later, it seems like I must have lived in a different family than they did. They don't remember the things that I do. We all agree about the city of Pittsburgh, though. Pittsburgh in the 1930s deserved its reputation of the Dirty City. Coal had been mined in the city since the mid-eighteenth century. Steel production began in 1875 and by 1911 Pittsburgh was producing as much as half of the nation's steel. By the early 1930s, during the economic depression that engulfed the nation, that flood had become a trickle. All around the city lines of smokestacks looked like huge dirty fingers jutting into the sky, their grey surfaces reflecting the dull detritus of smoke that had accumulated for years and years. Soft coal stoves dusted the atmosphere with a fine black soot, making everything it touched look grimy.

Along with the dirt and the smoke, Pittsburgh had all the other problems any other city had at that time. It seemed like nobody had jobs, most of us were on welfare. Franklin D. Roosevelt was like God, handing out food and clothes to us. We listened to the boxing matches on a neighbor's radio that she put outside when Joe Louis was boxing. Ma Barnes turned the volume as high as it would go, nobody seemed to mind, and we couldn't help but hear it anyway. We sat on our steps or the sidewalk or the curb near her house and cheered for Joe almost as loud as she did when he won, which he always did when I was listening. Life was a series of happenings: children died from diphtheria and scarlet fever; houses had signs on them warning neighbors about a contagious illness inside: yellow for diphtheria, red for scarlet fever, pink for measles, and white for some contagious disease that seemed too scary to ask about. Horses still hauled the garbage trucks, few cars went up or down our street; those that did were always black and decrepit looking.

Daddy's biggest complaint about Pittsburgh was that they took the pretty city of Allegheny, now the North Side, and ruined it by abandoning it. Before its annexation to the city of Pittsburgh in 1907, Allegheny City was an independent, thriving community with a healthy mix of wealthy and the working class.

Mama likened the land grab to our own loss of our house on Charles Street. Early in the Depression, our house was repossessed by the Savings and Loan Association because Mama could not meet the mortgage payments. We were allowed to live there but we had to pay rent to the bank. "Them dirty politicians! As bad as the bankers!" was her lament. In English! I guess it made her so mad she forgot to use the Irish.

A study of folklore
on the coast of Connacht, Ireland

Perhaps the wildest and least studied section of the wild western coasts of Ireland, the very fringe of the ancient world, are the shores and islands of the counties of Mayo and Galway. Even at the close of the 19th century one found districts little altered from the time when, two centuries before they had been described by the "chorographer", Roderic O'Flaherty, in his Hiar Connacht. "I myself," said he," have photographed the 'Cashlain Flaineen,' the charm intended to lure the shoals of fish within the nets, and have put turf on the Beltane fire. I have seen the canvas 'curragh' left adrift by poor people 'because it drowned a boy,' and the pipes left on the graves as an offering to the dead. I have seen the mirage of the lost islands, and heard the reputed wailing of the spirits of those lost at sea."

Christian writers spoke candidly about the Irish gods until the 10th century when European prejudice against Norse and Danish paganism led scholars to dispose of the old deities by turning them into human ancestors, and eventually into demons. These are the folk the peasants called the fairies.

25

Stories are told of fairy tricks such as 'fairy blight', an eddy of wind and dust that sometimes swirls about, carrying off the children. And of the Banshee, the fairy death goddess arriving with the howling of dogs and the creaking of furniture, who demanded her rightful place as first mourner to keen the death of a relation. Through the end of the 19th century these rituals were done and talked about boldly without hesitation. But by the time my mother and father left Ireland, the rites were done furtively and their power concealed from inquirers.

CHAPTER TWO

The Passage

I was never interested in going to Ireland; I had heard too much about the hard life there while I was growing up. But in 1988, when the opportunity arose, and our son and his family were going, I went. I find it difficult to describe my stay there and my feelings about meeting my parents' family for the first time. We came from Shannon airport on a modern four lane highway or 'dual carriageway', as they labeled it, and struggled through narrow, winding roads after we left Galway City toward the village of Lettermullen, a largish island connected by a bridge to the mainland.

It was raining, rain that felt like we were heading through a mist falling from the back of a thundering falls, hundreds of feet above. The rain lasted for two depressing days, then the sun penetrated the leftover mist and turned the grey rocks into soft shades of pale grey, verging on blue or green. Galway Bay looked almost blue with waves tipped with white instead of the grey, flat surface it had been; and on the mainland small plots of green separated by hedge rows, or low stone walls, rolled away from the sea.

It's hard to separate thoughts of the scenery from thoughts of the relatives. It only took a short time to realize that the O'Bearas, (Irish for Berry) my father's family, were barely on speaking terms with the McDonaghs, my mother's family. I expected to have great conversations with the many relatives that I had heard about who still lived in their village of Lettermullen, but most of the few relations that we met were wary and their aloofness kept me from asking questions that they would be reluctant to answer. Remarks like: "All those people (the McDonaghs) on the island were too fierce; they had too much ambition, they wanted everything in the world." Or "Johnny was a wild one and had none of the quietness of the O'Bearas." "They would have never married in Ireland," my cousin Mark, an O'Beara and my father's nephew, proclaimed and left me guessing. Were they both considered wild? Was there a lot of intermarriage out there at the edge of Connemara? There were an awful lot of McDonaghs for such a small place. But on the other hand, the Berrys were not so plentiful.

The O'Bearas of Connemara were ruddy, a heritage from the Spanish ancestors who were thrown on Ireland's rocky western coast four hundred years ago when ships from the Spanish Main were wrecked there. They were dark and quiet and seemed to have little patience with the light haired, light skinned families like my mother's who looked like the wild Norsemen that invaded Ireland in the distant past and became one with the native Celts.

We spent our days hiking around Lettermullen, wading through the tide pools, knocking barnacles off the rocks with a shovel to find some small, edible shellfish. We talked with people who apparently knew all about us before they came out of their cottages to greet us, and who then cheerfully explained how they were related to us, and made a few side remarks about one side or the other of my parents' families. I got little information from either side of the family other than the absolute fact that the McDonaghs did not make the poteen, the Irish bootleg liquor, any more. Which of course I knew was not true because of the 'vodka' bottles of the 'holy waters' that mysteriously showed up on the front step of our rented house each evening after supper. "Nobody lives on the island", my cousin Mark said. "You have to stay with it to make the poteen. They would never take the dole, you know. They have other ways to make their money."

The furtiveness and secrecy were part of that inheritance; added to the fact that my father came from the same village and, although not involved in the poteen traffic, entered America illegally. What a combination! Two people already schooled in the intricacies of secrecy joined together in a new world where prohibition was legal, and aliens could not reveal themselves.

In 1891 (or maybe 1892 or 1893 or 1894?), my mother

Bridget McDonough, (McDonagh in Irish) was born on a small island called Innisherk, off the coast of Connemara. She was the youngest of eleven children, all living in one small stone cottage. In 1988, I was stunned to learn that the house was still there, perched on top of a huge rock that slopes down to the Atlantic ocean. "Sure and it's the closest place to America." said my cousin Paddy, who rowed me over to the island in his curragh, the lightweight fishermen's boats that are still made by hand in Lettermullen. Only animals lived on the island by this time, and goats were tethered inside my mother's house. I felt offended, but politely kept quiet. After all I was a late visitor, a daughter arriving for the first time seventy years after her parents had left for good.

The main floor of my mother's house was divided in two, with a fireplace open on both sides about a third of the way across it. The smaller area was for the old folks and a loft above it was for the children.

There were no trees on the island; small tufts of stiff green grass of some sort peeked out from between the rocks which covered most of the ground. The families grew barley, using kelp as fertilizer, carried up from the sea in baskets.

The barley was used to make poteen, a form of whiskey that was bootlegged around the west coast and the Aran Islands. Mama's father probably had a curragh, part of the delivery system for the poteen. It was hard and heavy work, according to Mama. Once, in one of her unguarded moments, she said that her father was mean and made them work hard. She would say nothing further; one of those parent-children things like "ask me no questions and I'll tell you no lies," a constant response from Mama when we asked her questions. I wondered if her father was really a mean person? Or did he make them work because they had to find a way to get a living? Mama said another time that her father put money in a jug for the children to get passage to America and she was proud of the fact that she "had her passage", and didn't have to come to America in steerage.

Mama was a passenger on the last ship to come across the Atlantic before the first world war. The ship she came on, the Mauritania, was a sister to the Lusitania, which was sunk by the Germans soon after she arrived. She always said she didn't like Ireland and never wanted to go back there. She hated taking care of cows; carrying heavy baskets of kelp. She never gave other reasons, but she did go back twice before her marriage; the first time after her mother was kicked by a cow and died before Mama got there, and again when her father was ill. I think she made it that time before he died. It seems like such a little bit to know about her life before I knew her. I do know that she did not consider herself an immigrant; it was a word that I did not hear until I was grown.

Mama's brother Mike lived in East Pittsburgh. In order for her to come to America she had to have a sponsor and I think Uncle Mike did this for her. Her first job was as a maid somewhere in the East End of Pittsburgh but eventually she became the cook for people called Benz, a rich industrialist family also in the East End.

The young Irish immigrants went to the Irish dances on Saturday nights and I assume that's where Mama came in contact with Daddy again. I assume that because neither of them ever told us anything about their meeting.

Anyway, Mama always said that the Benz family was good to her. When she got married they gave her a set of carved glass bowls. They were beautiful but they didn't last long with a husband who threw things when he got drunk, and with six children who had no understanding of the value of them. I remember a picture that may have been of their wedding, Daddy looking very tall and Mama very small. None of the pictures seem to have lasted under our onslaught either. Many times Mama told us of all the nice furniture she had to sell during the depression and the glassware may have been part of that. But most of the photographs just got lost in the shuffle.

After they were married, Mama and Daddy lived in a house on Robinson Street on the lower North Side, then moved to another one on Arch Street, not many blocks away. There she established a rooming house for men who were new immigrants from Ireland; a common practice when men came alone to this country and needed a clean, safe place to sleep until they found a job and a wife.

The boarding house was a large, three story brick structure, with steps leading to the front door, where only the boarders could enter. We were not allowed even in the hallway, and the doors to our living space were always locked. Our entrance was the back door.

Mama took care of the boarders, cleaned the rooms, collected the rents, made sure they kept their place. To me, those men were almost a myth. I never saw any of them. Mama was wary of "them Irish men", and kept them away from us.

Mama's hair was a blondish red, the color that makes you look like you have no eyebrows. Her eyes were bright blue. She worked during the week at one job or another, scrubbing floors at Montefiore Hospital and for people in Squirrel Hill, a section of Pittsburgh, until sometime in the late forties, when she started working as a cook in various restaurants. On Sundays she invariably slept most of the afternoon on the couch with a newspaper over her head. Why? I am shrugging my shoulders as I write. To keep the light off? To let us know not to bother her?

As hard as I try to remember Mama when I was little, I can't see her face. I can feel her presence, I can remember some of her clothes: the black, Cuban heeled shoes that were always hurting her feet; the black straw hat that she wore to church; the big purse that she kept in the cupboard in the sideboard, the one on the right side, (the left one was for new kittens), the small flowers in the dresses she wore at home; the apron that she put over her head through a hole in the material and tied behind her back; the motion of carefully getting her bush of hair through the opening. Sometimes a hair pin would catch on the edge of the apron hole and she would move her head slightly to unhook it. Her arms looked big, heavy above the elbows, with firm forearms, big, solid hands. As she tied the apron strings in back she was already looking at whatever came next. Mama never just sat, except when she was sad or worrying.

Daddy was born in Lettermullen, and his family was considered to be part of the elite of Western Ireland. A monument in front of the Star of the Sea Church in Lettermullen is dedicated to the people who built the boats "out of their head," and Daddy's family was one of them. His family may have been elite, but they were less practical than Mama's and more inclined to solve their problems with drink.

There are, or were, two kinds of drinkers in Ireland: the ones who can drink as much as they want and still be able to function well, and the ones who after the first drink became immediately non-functional. Bridget's family, the McDonaghs, were one of the former, and Johnny's, the O'Beara's, was one of the latter. Both descendents of the Celts in western Ireland, and of the fierce people Oliver Cromwell pushed to the sea "where   there's no tree to hang them and no ground to bury them" who were never truly conquered by the English. They are also descendents of the Vikings, who invaded in the tenth century, and the Moors who landed on the western coast in the sixteenth century. The Vikings seem to have had more tolerance for alcohol than the Celts and perhaps the Moors. That's my theory, anyway, having observed both traits in my family: Mama the typical Viking and Daddy the typical Celt and maybe Moor. Another of my theories, based on observation of Mama and Daddy, is that you cannot ignore an intelligent, creative, mind. You must find a way to engage it or you will depart mentally from the world. This I believe is part of the Irish passion for education.

About thirty years ago, when I was a student at Seton Hill College for my undergraduate degree, I wrote a research paper about Irish families in America. The part that I remember most clearly was about the attitudes toward drinking alcohol. In Ireland drinking was looked upon as simply part of the culture. But in America, it became something to be looked down upon.

After that, I began to think about my father differently. I was able to see him as what the Irish call a "lovely man." He was big and handsome, gentle and humorous, adventurous and smart. The only time that he showed any anger or violence was when he got extremely drunk. Then Mama would yell at him for coming home like that and he would pick up a pot or a dish and throw it on the floor, say something in Irish and leave. One time Mama said he had broken up her whole kitchen and left her with the mess; part of the reason maybe, that Daddy stayed away so long when he was drinking.

We never talked about Daddy when he wasn't there; never talked about him at all, actually. Mama never said anything in English anyway. Of course we assumed from the tone of her voice that she was saying things that she didn't want us to hear. It seemed to me he always came home when she wasn't there or when he was completely sober, or if he knew his brother was coming. Uncle Eddie never touched the stuff and had a very stern wife who ruled her family like a tyrant.

When Daddy finally did come home after one of his binges, he would arrive very quietly. He avoided Mama and Mary, too, because she showed her anger when she saw him. But I never said anything, so he did not send me out of the room. At those times he went into the kitchen, heated a can of chile con carne and carried it out to the porch in warm weather or into the middle room by the stove fire in the winter.

"Don't tell your mother I'm home," was all he said. But she always knew and said, "Well, he's home."

I always knew that Daddy liked me. He called me by pet names: Clara Bow, or Anna Held, both silent movie stars. He would point to the picture of St. Theresa of the Little Flower and say that was me. Mama said he took Mary for walks and played with her when she was little and took her on street car rides when she was older. But she had a different attitude toward him later. By that time she was 'on Mama's side' and remained there. I didn't know whose side I was on. I think I just watched, puzzled and confused. I couldn't take sides.

I often wandered into the living room or the porch where Daddy was sitting, wearing a plaid wool shirt if it was cold or long sleeved underwear if it was warm. No matter what time of year it was he wore black pants. It may have been the same pair, I don't know. Nobody washed wool at that time and I can't remember ever going to a cleaner's. He always had something to read in his hand, a newspaper, a book one of us had left lying about, even an encyclopedia from a set Mary had been given by somebody at school, would write in Irish in the columns of the books he read. He had a gentle voice and sang Irish songs almost under his breath. He did tell stories, but not to me; he told them when he and his brothers and Mama's brothers and nephews were sitting around in the kitchen. Many of these stories were related to me by others. He told some of them to Joe. He took care of Joe a lot when he was little and the rest of us were at school. I think Joe loved Daddy and identified with him. But Joe, being a lot like Daddy, didn't tell us many of the stories either. Most of the time we heard them first from our cousin Eddie, who got them from his father, Uncle Eddie Berry.

A true story, confirmed by British Naval records, is that Uncle Eddie crossed the ocean to Canada as a sailor and then "ran," the English equivalent of jumping ship. This was at a time early in the twentieth century when the Irish Republican Army was forcing young men to join or hide to save their lives. Daddy never told anyone how he got here, but he spent a lot of time with Uncle Eddie traveling around the northern part of the country, and I decided that he must have been a stowaway. He did occasionally give us a few words about some of his travels: riding the rails; working in a copper mine in Montana and avoiding an explosion which killed many men because he and Uncle Eddie were drunk and couldn't get up for work. My cousin Eddie verified this story and there is a history of the mine explosion, so it is believable.

Daddy also talked about riding the street car between Pittsburgh and Chicago. According to a history of street cars found in the Pittsburgh Historical Society, this could also be true. Amusement parks, including Kennywood near Pittsburgh, built trolley lines to all of the small communities along that route and built amusement parks there.

I can see my father's face very clearly; the way his eyebrows delineated his forehead, moved, jutted out, his dark eyes, his bigness, his hands always holding something: a book, a pot of tea, a can of chili; his baggy pants, his plaid shirt, his cap, his giant step kind of walk. He often sat in a large chair with his legs crossed, reading or crooning some Irish melody, or just sitting.

I realize now that I loved both of my parents, but I never talked about them when they were alive. Secrecy was necessary for survival here in America, where our parents had to make sure that they made their living honestly. Or at the very least, they had to keep the appearance of it. In America the world was much larger; secrecy more difficult to promise. No wonder we had to be very, very good in America. Our parents had to make sure that they kept their secrets to themselves.

A short history of Immigration and Welfare

From 1892 to 1954 over twelve million immigrants entered the United States, most of them through Ellis Island, the small island in New York Harbor within the shadow of the Statue of Liberty. First and second class passengers were not required to undergo the inspection process unless they were sick or had legal problems, the theory being that if people could afford to purchase a first or second class ticket, they were less likely to become a public charge.

The government felt that more affluent passengers would not end up in institutions, hospitals or become a burden to the state.

This scenario was far different for "steerage" or third class passengers. These immigrants traveled in crowded and often unsanitary conditions near the bottom of steamships with few amenities, often spending up to two weeks seasick in their bunks during rough Atlantic crossings.

After World War I, prospective immigrants began applying for their visas at American consulates in their countries of origin. The necessary paperwork and a medical inspection were conducted there.

The death knell for immigration began between the passage of Quota laws in 1921 and the passage of the National Origins Act in 1924. These restrictions were based on a percentage system according to the number of ethnic groups already living in the United States as per the 1890 and 1910 census.

Many of the immigrants were poor. The poorest of the poor were aided by private organizations, churches and occasionally by small state programs.

In 1933, as part of his New Deal, President Roosevelt created Aid to Families with Dependent Children (AFDC). Essentially, individuals had to qualify for benefits by demonstrating need and by maintaining minimal assets of their own.

In the beginning, this program was designed to be a short-term, transitional solution to the problems faced by single poor women with children, many of whom were immigrants as well. Small cash benefits were offered to recipients, although the recipients were monitored by caseworkers who had a lot of leeway in determining who would receive benefits and how much they would get.

Although recipients were not expected to work, some Americans soon protested that these individuals were taking advantage of the system and that the benefits awarded to them were undeserved. The AFCD program quickly became the most stigmatizing welfare program to evolve from the New Deal and became known as " welfare."

In 1935 a bill containing the original provisions for AFDC was signed by President Roosevelt and created the basic structure of the modern welfare.

CHAPTER THREE

The Greenhorn

Our parents came over during the great Irish migration before 1926. Mama said that she came over in 1914 and had her own "passage," meaning that she had a ticket and had a cabin and could move about the ship as she pleased. Apparently she was not among the millions who came to the United States through Ellis Island; she talked only about Boston, without really telling us that's where she arrived. "They didn't like the Irish in Boston," was one of the comments that led me to believe that.

I know that Daddy came earlier than 1914 that but how, when or where is a mystery. By the time our cousin Delia came over, sometime in the mid 1930s, there were only a trickle of immigrants. There seemed to be a lot of relatives going and coming from our house before that, but she was the last one to come. "A plague to all of us." Mama said. Especially to me, as it turned out.

Welfare was a savior for us; it gave us food. The powdered milk was undrinkable but Mama used it in cooking. The oleo had to be mixed with a little orange packet of color, usually by me or Betty, but other than that the food was good, especially the fruit.

We also got clothes from the welfare. That did not work as well. We had to go to one store in downtown Pittsburgh, the name of which I forget, maybe purposely. We had to take what they gave us: coats one or two sizes larger than we wore, shoes that had paper under the soles, found when a hole appeared in the sole of a shoe after a short time of wearing it. Everything was dark blue, black or brown. Daddy once came with us and he got a jacket that was supposed to be leather, what kind nobody knew. A few days after we got it home it gave out a horrible smell.

"I think they gave me the camel," he said when he threw

it away. That was the last time he went to get clothes. They did not give money. I could not figure out how the rent was paid, although at the time I never thought of it. Mama worked at menial jobs and Daddy got some work on the WPA, one of Roosevelt's programs to provide jobs. He brought some of this money home then, causing arguments with Mama about what he did with the rest of it, probably left in a saloon with the "bums" down on the North Side.

Our uncles were visiting. Not Mama's brothers; they hardly ever came, we had to go and visit them if Mama wanted to see them, but Daddy's brothers: Uncle Eddie and Uncle Mike and their brother from Chicago, Uncle Pat. Mary, Betty and I listened to them telling secrets in Irish and watched Mama flute the top of pie crusts; her left hand pinching the top and bottom crusts together while she made little waves on the edges with her right. I liked the way her fingers seemed to be dancing, the movement quick and light, in spite of their heavy look. It was still a major event for us to have apple pie; we could not afford that many apples before we started getting a bushel of them every week from the welfare.

Daddy and the Uncles sat on kitchen chairs, wooden ones that had been yellow at one time but were now a muddy mustard color. Elbows on their knees, feet flat on the floor, twirling their caps on one finger, they faced away from Mama in their own circle. "You know the greenhorn is coming," Daddy said.

Mama's fingers stopped; she looked over at the Uncles and said something in the Irish. Daddy's hands became quiet, the cap motionless. He turned around and looked at me.

"Sure, now," he said, "you have heard of the fairies?" It was a question but I guess he didn't expect an answer because he started talking again. "There are strange beings in Ireland," he said. "They come out of the mist and like to hide among the grass and trees." He was silent for so long that I leaned over the back of the chair, nudging his shoulder as I did so and he began again.

"Sometimes they lost their way and landed in Connemara. When they have something to hide behind they are just mischievous." Again he was quiet for a few minutes. I made myself wait; nudging would not work twice.

"They like the middle and the east part of Ireland where there are lots of trees and grass," he continued. "There's no trees in the West, where we were, just rocks that cover the land and go out to the sea and turn black from the tides coming in. So the poor fairies had no place to hide and if you caught them they were likely to get mean."

I had heard about fairies but this was the first time Daddy had talked about them. I thought about them the way I thought about God and the Blessed Mother; everybody talked about them but nobody ever saw them.

"Well now," Daddy said. The uncles had stopped twirling their caps and were watching my father as if he was the priest telling the gospel.

"We had the spirits who were always leaving their graves. And no wonder. The poor things, they were buried too close to the rocks and the sea and liked to wander. We got used to them, they didn't bother us. But they did not like mischief and would go after them fairies. So the creatures would grow horns on their heads to protect themselves."

"That's enough of that!" Mama interrupted. "Don't be making up stories!" She put the last pie in the oven and slammed the door to emphasize her words. "Tell her that the greenhorn is just one of them people that are coming over from Ireland to make a decent living here." Daddy and the uncles went back to twirling their caps. I would hear no more from him about the fairies.

For days afterward, I could almost see the greenhorn; not a person but a wispy monster with a horn sticking out of his head like the unicorn in the stories at school. He would come into our treeless neighborhood, lunging at people and rip them apart with his ferocious weapon.

A week later my sister Betty and I were kneeling on

chairs playing with cutouts spread across the kitchen table that was big enough for the eight chairs that we needed, plus two more for company. We were drawing clothes for dolls that our cousin Jean had drawn, colored and cut out for us. The doorbell rang, something that didn't happen very often since Mama stuck a pin in it because the neighborhood kids thought it was such fun to ring it every time one of them went by our house. We dropped the cutouts and dived under the table, our favorite listening post. Betty was willing to go along with anything that I wanted to do and we often pretended it was our cave. Sometimes Mama even forgot that we were there.

"It's the greenhorn!" I whispered, trying to sound brave but peeking out to see the creature. A small pale face peeked out from hair sprung out like a huge red halo around its head. It carried a suitcase that bulged in odd places that immediately scared me more. What was causing those strange shapes? And the creature wore a dress. A dress! One just like my mother wore to church on Sundays, dark blue silky material with a small flower design all over, overflowing onto the same black, sturdy looking shoes. It was a girl greenhorn! She had no horns that I could see but maybe she had some way of hiding them. Her eyes, bright blue like Mama's, darted from one place to another, finally focusing on the table where I had stuck my head out far enough to see.

"What in the name of God are you doing there?" Her first words came out in the familiar brogue of my mother and father, and the same demanding tone as Mama had when we were being disobedient.

"Get out of there, now," Mama commanded, yanking my arm and pulling me to my feet. "This is your cousin Delia."

Delia stared at me until I looked away, unable to speak. I thought about her a lot, though. Delia, her rigid, stocky figure, eyes unblinking, freckles covering her pale skin, was an immigrant like the many others who had come to our house, but she was different; she stayed longer. And she had none of that humility that I thought anybody who came to live with us should have. It didn't help that Mama complained about her for not giving us any money. "She had her passage, didn't she?" Mama would say. "My brother paid for her to come across and gave her money, now, too. I wish to God I had never been that good to her." Years later I remembered Mama's words and silently agreed with her.

One Sunday Mama and I went to visit Uncle Mike, Mama's brother. Delia was supposed to come but had some excuse: "Hmmff!" Mama growled. "Well, she will have to find her own way. Not wanting to see her own uncle that she has not seen for years!" We went by streetcar, a dark yellow wooden car with huge metal wheels that moved on tracks in the center of streets all over Pittsburgh. There was a long pole that connected the car to an overhead electric power line, and the car swayed with any wind that happened to move the air above it, causing weak stomached people like me to get sick and throw up on the floor, then walk off, leaving the mess for somebody else to clean up and try again on the next car that came along.

That day, I made the mistake of wearing my yellow dress. East Pittsburgh was the epicenter of Pittsburgh's mills and smokestacks. None of the mills were working at that time, but the air was still full of black particles that clung to everything they touched. Years later soft coal was banned and we had to use charcoal bricks of hard coal from eastern Pennsylvania. How I hated those lumps that took forever to catch fire and whose flames were dull compared to the bright orange and deep yellow ones of our own western Pennsylvania coal. But it left a dirty legacy that Pittsburgh will always be remembered for.

The street car ran along the river and stopped at every block. By the time we got off the street car and walked up the hill to my uncle's house my dress was stiff with dried vomit and the wet skirt gathered even more black soot than the rest of the dress. Uncle Mike's wife tried to wipe it off but just made it worse, probably because I didn't like the way she ordered me to sit down so she could clean it, and I wouldn't sit still. Also, I knew that she was his second wife and she didn't act like the

Irish women I knew, so I was suspicious of her. I liked his house, though. It had a big porch and a swing hanging by two chains from the porch ceiling. It was almost as big as our house and nice and clean and orderly, because nobody else lived there with them, which seemed strange to me. There were always a lot of people in our house and it seemed like the other houses on our street were the same.

I had to sit on the streetcar for an hour on the way home, praying my stomach would not rebel again. Passing the rows of smokestacks that stood black and neglected on the way home, Mama never failed to say "Ora musha", the Irish words for "oh my," that she used when she felt sad, causing me to feel sad, too, without knowing the reason.

How to make Root Beer from extract

Buy some root beer extract and follow the instructions, dissolving sugar into boiling water and adding the extract. Pour the flavored sugar water into a container that can be covered. When the liquid temperature is warm (about 75F degrees), add a package of yeast. Over the next twelve hours the yeast will continue to eat, and huge amounts of carbonation and foam will result, and then subside. Bacteria can easily contaminate the root beer and make it taste nasty, so keep it clean and covered. It is the process of fermentation that puts the little bubbles (carbon dioxide), into the root beer. After the initial carbonation subsides (about twelve hours), you can bottle it!

CHAPTER FOUR

Delia's Story

Since Mama brought Delia over, she had to find a job for her. This was 1936 and the depression was as bad as ever. Even the rich people in the East End, the traditional employers of Irish girls, weren't hiring. So Delia was sitting - "mooning around", as Mama said - with nothing to do except to go to the Irish dances held in the Catholic church basement, where she was sure to meet some lazy Irishman. So Mama decided that Delia could watch us when she had to go to work and Daddy was not at home. Mama scrubbed floors at Montefiore Hospital and worked in the evenings and late into the night.

In our daily life Mary, the oldest, took on the responsibility of caring for the family when Mama was not at home. Jackie, as the oldest son, ignored her orders. I resented being told what to do and usually found a way to disappear with a book when Mary was in charge.

It was a big relief for me not to have to watch Betty. I hated having to do it. She was cute with blond hair and brown eyes that were so nearsighted that she had to get close to whatever she was looking at, so she always seemed to be leaning over you when she talked to you. She didn't get glasses until she started to school. She was old enough to do what she was supposed to do, but she never did, and nobody ever did anything about it. If she started to grab things and holler Mama just said to take her somewhere out of the way. Even when we played cards with Daddy, we couldn't play Euchre because Betty got mad when we told her she did something wrong. Daddy said she was too young and the game was too hard for her, so we had to play Old Maid. Betty never sat on a chair. She knelt and leaned over the table, trying to look into everybody's hands. Her hair would have been nice, it was curly like Shirley Temple's, not wiry like Mama's, but she pulled at it and messed it up with her dirty hands. She was always dirty, no matter how much we tried to clean her up. I couldn't understand how she got along in school, even in second grade the Sisters expected better behavior.

It was Saturday morning. I had finished scrubbing the kitchen floor; Mary had done the dishes and we were in the kitchen trying to get the tangles out of Betty's hair and make her wash her hands and face. Delia was sitting on the marble seat in the hall looking at herself from every direction in the mirror.

"That's all she ever does," I complained.

"She must think she's pretty," Mary said. Mary had curly black hair and green eyes and was smaller than me even if she was two years older. She had everything I wished I had: she was twelve and was pretty and allowed to go places with Daddy and all the sisters at school liked her because she was smart and never got sick and missed school. I had straight brown hair and my eyes didn't know whether to be blue or brown. Daddy tried to make me feel good once by telling me they were hazel, a color I decided he made up because I had never heard of it before. And I missed school all the time because I got sick a lot.

"No," I said, "she's looking for pimples. I saw her squeezing one last week when she thought no one was around."

"Anyway," said Betty, pushing her yellow curls out of her eyes, leaving a dark streak of dirt on her cheek. She was kneeling on the chair, rocking it back and forth until it looked like it would tumble her to the floor. "When Mama and Daddy are not home Delia is supposed to be watching us, not herself."

Delia was bossy. She stood with her hands on her hips the way Mama did and was always telling us what to do. Now she was saying that we could not go to the story hour at the Carnegie Library, that lovely time when we listened to stories about fairies and witches and beautiful princesses and brave princes.

"Mama always let us go," Mary argued.

"I'm telling you for the last time," Delia said, "you're too little now, to be going down there by yourself."

"I want to hear stories," Betty started to cry. "If you

46

don't let us go to the library I'll tell Daddy you drank some of the root beer before it was done."

Mary looked at me as if to say: "We got her!" I was astonished that Delia would have done that. Daddy made root beer in the big crock in the cellar sometimes and if the top was taken off too soon the root beer would be flat and taste awful.

Delia's face got red and she was quiet for a long time, then she got up, went into the living room and sat down on the rocker. Betty, still crying, pounded on the arm and yelled: "You're sitting on Mama's rocker! We never sit on Mama's rocker!"

I pulled Betty away from Delia and held her. "Delia is allowed to," I told her. She put her thumb in her mouth, sniffled some more and climbed up beside me on the couch.

"I can tell you some stories about Ireland," Delia suddenly announced. "If you don't tell on me," she added.

"About Mama and Daddy?" We never heard much about their life in Ireland, they only said things like how mean the English were or how hard it was to live there.

"People over in Ireland said I was just like your mother," she said.

"Our mother?" I looked at her with surprise. How could she be like Mama, I thought. She did look like her, though, with her red hair; and she was built the same, sort of chunky looking. But Mama laughed and talked with everybody, sometimes even with Daddy when he was sober. She did things with us, took us to the show, bought us ice cream cones when we went to get clothes at the welfare. Delia never smiled and never did anything for us and I had never even seen her wash a dish or sweep the floor. But with a possible story, even from Delia, I was not going to say anything that would stop her.

"Your mother is my mother's sister," she said. "Your grandmother was my grandmother, your mother is my aunt."

I was familiar with aunts, but a grandmother! "I never knew I had a grandmother," I said.

Betty pulled her thumb out of her mouth. "There's a

wicked stepmother in Snow White," she said and wiping her thumb on her dress.

"No," I said, "that's different, that's just a fairy tale. And she's not a grandmother."

But it was puzzling. "Are there any grandmothers living around here?" I asked Mary. None of the kids on our block ever mentioned any. "I don't know," she answered.

"Sure and everybody has a grandmother." Delia said.

"Why doesn't she come to see us?" I asked.

Betty was sucking her thumb again. "Take your thumb out of your mouth!" Delia commanded. Betty stared at her and sucked harder, burying her head against my shoulder. "I'm seven" she whispered. "I'm not sucking my thumb."

"She can't come to see you now, God save us," Delia went on. "She was out in the pasture one morning with the cow and it kicked her. Now, I never heard of a cow kicking somebody to death, but this one did and before we knew what was happening she was dead and buried." Delia blessed herself. "She's in heaven now, God willing."

We heard this in silence. As a story, it didn't seem worth keeping her secret about the root beer, especially if one of us got the blame for it.

"That's not a story!" Betty took her thumb out of her mouth. "It's too short," she said and looked at Mary for confirmation. "Is it?" she asked. Mary was the oldest and knew about almost everything.

"I think it's a different kind of story, Betty," she said after some thought. "It's not a fairy tale but maybe a true story. Is it, Delia?"

"I wouldn't be telling you one of them fairy stories, now would I? Now, I won't say strange things don't happen. There's shiny black seals that sit on the rocks and you can see them sometimes through the mist. They do say they become women if you catch them, but I never heard of anyone catching one." Betty's mouth opened and her thumb settled on her lower lip. "And", Delia continued, "when the waves come up high by the cottage you can hear them roaring like the devil was coming for you. Your mother's cottage is on a big rock that goes down to meet the ocean. Some say there is a spirit down there that never lets the sea get into the house."

"Is it true what you are saying?" Mary asked. Mary never talked like that, in the Irish way of words and almost sounding like she was singing. Mama probably would have corrected her if she heard it saying: "You sound like you just came over on the last boat," the worst thing you could say about a person who was trying to be American in every way.

"Is it true?" mimicked Delia. "How would you be knowing if a thing is true or not? The cottages have walls so thick that you're two steps into the house before you see the room and there are no doors or windows on the ocean side to keep the waves from coming in."

"Did you live in the Grandmother's house?" I asked.

"No, I did not," she said, "but there were only seven cottages on the island and I lived right next to it. I always liked to go there."

"What was her house like?" I loved to hear about houses and beautiful furniture and gorgeous clothes.

"It was just a cottage like everybody lives in. There was glass in the windows, all of us on the island had that while some in Connemara did not. There was not a lot of light though. We had no windows on the ocean side and the English did not allow big windows, God alone knows why, but there it is. We had floors, too, not dirt like some of them other Irish had, but stones smooth and even."

"What was it like inside?" asked Mary.

"It was nice and peaceful," Delia said in a sort of dreamy voice. "And clean. The old people were strict about the cleaning."

"She sounds like Mama," I said. I had suffered many sore bottoms for not scrubbing the kitchen floor well enough.

Mary was persistent. "But what was it like inside?" she asked again.

"I guess it was much like my house, except that my

mother didn't clean as much but she did make it look pretty inside." That dreamy look again. "Nobody else on the island painted the inside walls of their cottages, but she painted hers yellow. She painted blue and white squares around the fireplace and wouldn't put anything on the walls except pictures of trees and grass. Her mother tried to get her to put up a picture of the Sacred Heart and she wouldn't do it. She did have a statue of the blessed Mother above the fireplace, though. That's who she prayed to." She stopped again. I was waiting for that look to turn into a smile but she just said: "Betty is almost asleep."

"All that crying and carrying on did it." I said. "I'll just put her on the couch."

"She's such a baby," Mary said later. "That's the first time Delia has told us anything and she had to go and spoil it." I didn't say anything but I thought, if Betty hadn't threatened her with telling about the root beer we would not have had any story at all. We would still be sitting around complaining about Delia. Mama never said much about the island except things like: "There was nothing but only the sea and the rocks," and "I would never go back." I could imagine the devilish waves flinging themselves up at the house, furious because there were no windows to let the devil in. No wonder her mother wanted color in her house. I would have wanted color, too, if the whole world seemed grey and cloudy like the ocean. Maybe color kept the devil out, too.

Memorial Day Parade

In my new blue dress
with the big white collar
I followed the parade to the cemetery
where soldiers were honored
by friends and families.

I stopped and stood alone
while the band moved on.
In the silence I touched
the white marble of the headstones
saw the sky through sun trapped leaves
glowing far above
smelled the fragrance of the flowers
blooming on the graves
sat on the damp grass, traced the names
carved on the rough surface of a marker.

I felt privileged to be in this place
usually locked in behind high black gates
which guard those lonely spirits
from the drab streets
where they lived their lives.

Movie Attendance in the 1930s

The economic downturn of the Depression was precipitated by a rapid decline in values of stock at the New York Stock Exchange in the fall of 1929. The economy continued to decline through 1932. Between 1929 and 1932, when Franklin Roosevelt assumed the presidency, national income was cut in half, five thousand banks collapsed, and over nine million savings accounts evaporated.

Inevitably, such an economic climate hit Hollywood hard. The industry had enjoyed a period of prosperity in the 1920s, but between 1930 and 1933, movie attendance and industry revenues dropped. Total company profits of fifty four and a half million dollars in 1929 gave way to losses of almost fifty six million dollars in 1932. MGM was the only large studio that continued to make a profit. Smaller companies survived in part by making "B" movies that were shown as double features.

Some theater owners began to offer giveaway programs, like 'dish night' or games of chance. SCREENO, a variety of Bingo, was the most popular.

Box office receipts bottomed out in 1933, and gradually improved for the rest of the decade.

CHAPTER FIVE

Telling Dresses

Mama finally got Delia a job keeping house for a doctor who lived in the fancier part of the North Side.

"Thank God and the Blessed Mother!" Mama said when she got home after talking to the doctor. "She's got a room to live in there, too. I thought she would never leave us alone. Much good it will do him, though. She never did a stitch of work here."

"Do you think she ever did a stitch of work in Ireland?" I asked.

Mama clicked her tongue, a sound that she made when she didn't like something. "Her mother was never much for housekeeping," she said.

"Why? What was her mother like? Delia said that her grandmother and our grandmother were the same person."

"Hmmpf," Mama said, "Ask me no questions and I'll tell you no lies," her usual answer when one of us asked questions she didn't want to answer. She raised her eyebrows; they were so light you couldn't see them unless she did that and brought them out from behind the tops of the glasses. "We'll say no more about it," she said and clicked her tongue again.

"Mama," I said, "why don't you teach Betty to make that noise? Maybe she could do that instead of yelling." Mary laughed and Mama glared at me.

Looking back on that small conversation I wonder why Mama would not talk about her mother.

I don't have a way to explain about my lack of a concept of grandmothers when I was little. Maybe a grandmother is like love, if you don't experience it it's difficult to understand and conceive of it. Now as a grandmother myself, I understand that children need and appreciate what grandmothers can give them; words and actions that fill up the spaces between parent care and learning about the world and understanding their heritage.

Our neighborhood was filled with immigrants whose parents were still in the old country of their origin so that there actually were no grandparents. They may have been there, but I didn't recognize them. Even though I was an avid observer of the neighbors, I seldom talked to them. People seemed to move so often from one neighborhood to another, maybe because many of them were renters moving to find a cheaper place to live; maybe because most of them were like us: poor and ashamed of it, maybe they were on welfare and didn't want to let people know, maybe they were not used to trusting anybody. I was shy and I knew nothing about those who did not come outside and sit on their steps or porches, and my mother's strict rule was that we were not allowed to talk to the neighbors. We were warned from the time we could talk not to tell people anything about our family. My mother didn't talk about her family because, I now understand, they were considered lawless. The neighbors may have had the same rule. I had no way of judging them, only a vague longing for something, but I didn't know what. It was just the way it was. But I don't think I ever saw a grandmother sitting outside.

I never thought about Mama's mother as a grandmother, but only as a figure in an intriguing story. Later I learned that my grandmother's mother and most of her family were deported to Australia by the British during the disastrous potato famine of the 1850s in Ireland. At twelve years of age, Nora Lee, my grandmother, was left behind on the island to take care of her old grandfather.

I imagined her with Mama's blue eyes and wild, red hair, racing around the island making poteen and ordering the men back to their boats when they tried to drink on the island. "We'll have no drinking here and have ye drowning, trying to swim your way back!" I couldn't figure out how a cow could kill her by kicking her, and now I wonder if it had something to do with those drunken men. This history may also have something to do with the fact that there was no drinking allowed in our house. Even when Daddy's brothers visited, Mama's greeting was always "Ar mhaith leat cupan tae?" (which sounded like shirn cupon tay) which means, "Would a cup of tea be good with you?" Mama did make hot toddies (hot tea laced with whiskey) for us when we were sick though, so how can I explain that? Maybe she had a secret stash somewhere for such emergencies, but I know I never found it.

I imagine how Nora must have felt when she was left alone to take care of herself and the old man. If she was anything like Mama, she would have bitter, angry memories of her family, she would have hated the island. According to contemporary history, the meager Connemara soil would only support a little barley and the English gave them little food. So Nora and the grandfather and the few others left on the island would have done the only thing possible, use the barley to make the poteen, sell it to those on nearby islands, or barter it for food on the mainland. "Damn them all!" she would say, just like Mama damned the politicians who, she said, took our house away when she could not make the payments, turning us into renters without land or a house of our own.

The boarding house that Mama had when she was first married was rented, but she was determined to have a house of her own. She saved enough money for a down payment on the house on Charles Street and we moved there a year before the depression started. I remembered the Arch Street boarding house as bright and cheerful with lots of windows. All of our rooms were on one floor, the kitchen was warm, and we knew that Mama was upstairs somewhere cleaning the rooms for the boarders. This was in deep contrast to the house on Charles Street, which seemed dark and forbidding. "We should have kept the boarding house", Mama sometimes said.

Nighttime was fantasy time for Mary, Betty and I. Mary always loved clothes. When I went to the movies I worried about the heroine and her hero and knew the whole story. When Mary went to the movies, she remembered every piece of clothing that the women and girls wore. I paid no attention to this until the three of us had to sleep in the attic and Mary came up with the idea of talking about dresses and clothes.

We slept in the front attic room, all the way to the third floor. The only light was in the ceiling, and nobody was willing to get up and turn it off after reading for a while, so we didn't even turn it on. Instead, we would lay in the dark and talk. Mama could not hear us up there. The fantasies that we shared came from our longings for all the things that we saw in movies and movie magazines, the things we couldn't afford, and knew we would never have. So we called them 'stories', something we were used to hearing and did not need to be true. I think we didn't realize how much of Mama and Daddy's life was kept from us, and how we kept our secrets from each other, too.

Every night Betty would say:" Let's tell dresses!" and then promptly fall asleep as Mary and I dreamt out loud. The stories became tales of what we would do if we were beautiful and had money and handsome men falling in love with us.

Mary would start with a description of some dress she had seen Joan Crawford or Deanna Durbin wear in a recent movie. It would usually be beautiful silk or satin material and she would describe the color as if she had actually seen it, which was impossible in a black and white movie. "Remember," she would say, "the dress Joan Crawford wore when she came down the steps into the living room?" Or the dining room? Or the porch? Joan was always floating down some set of fabulous stairs.

I would imagine the dress in my mind and tell about the accessories, shiny black or red patent leather shoes with diamond buckles on the front. There would be purses studded with diamonds or emeralds and fur coats of ermine or mink to drape over our shoulders. We fantasized about how we would wear those lovely clothes when we would be movie stars, gracefully making a grand entrance into some ballroom, or waltzing in the spotlight of a stage with glamorous people applauding us.

Betty, and later my littlest sister Margie, must have felt safe when Mary and I spun fantasy stories by the hour and conjured a new way of talking to each other. Thinking back, the sound of our voices probably comforted them. Those nights talking and listening to each other gave us a sense of closeness that we did not have otherwise.

When Mary didn't feel like talking I would go back to imagining the neighborhood in my mind, mapping house by house. Even now I love to see the inside of other people's houses; how they decorate them, how the kitchen is arranged, what kind of pictures are on the walls. Ours always had holy pictures; the Sacred Heart, St. Theresa and a picture made of aluminum foil that Jackie made when he was in fifth or sixth grade. I was never invited into any of our neighbors houses, but most of them did a lot of living outside on the steps, so I had to make do with that.

We were not allowed to play with our neighbors, the Nicotras, or maybe they were not allowed to play with us. They were noisy and sang at night when they were sitting out on the six steps to their front door. I could hear them from our bedroom window and wished I could sit on their bottom step and hear the things that made them laugh. Next door to them lived the Dailys, an Irish family who were unfriendly. The "shanty Irish," Mama called them and we were warned to ignore them. She said they came from some part of Ireland where the people were careless and poor and didn't try to be anything better.

A couple of doors up from them lived an Indian girl, a real American Indian. Helen always walked down the street with her head down, not looking at anybody. We never saw her parents, but I imagined that her house was filled with bows and arrows and soft buffalo hides. Maybe the grandmother stayed in the house and chewed on the skins to make them soft. Helen had skin that was darker than ours, but not red like people said was the color of Indians.

We never invited anybody to our house. I was afraid to because Daddy would come in drunk and I could never be sure how he would act. He might be nice like he was to me or yell like he did with Mama and sometimes Jackie.

Jackie was a year older than me, in between Mary and

me, and I was never sure how he would act, either. He teased a lot. I didn't mind because I knew he liked me but other kids might not like it. Mary was worse than me about how Daddy might act. She would get angry and say things out loud to Mama like: "How could we ever invite anybody into this house with him around?" Betty just didn't care; she wasn't old enough yet to worry about friends.

Rita's house was the last one on our block. It had a front yard with a low wooden fence around it. Mama didn't object to Rita, maybe because Mama talked to her mother and sometimes went to church with her. Rita was younger than me and didn't go out of her yard much, and never came down Charles Street, so we would talk to her when she was in her yard. Her mother came out sometimes and smiled and talked to me. She looked old, and Rita called her Mamere, which I thought was another way of saying Mama. Now that I think about it, maybe she was Rita's grandmother.

The Irish Wake

The Irish wake is one of the best known funeral traditions associated with Ireland. The wake, the glorious send-off of departed loved ones, is a prominent feature of Irish funeral traditions, but is seen less and less often in modern Ireland and is now almost unknown in the cities.

The origin of the wake probably dates back to the ancient Jewish custom of leaving the sepulcher, or burial chamber, of a recently departed relative, unsealed for three days before finally closing it up, during which time family members would visit frequently in the hope of seeing signs of a return to life.

A more recent story, which is almost certainly a myth, is that the tradition of the wake in Ireland came about as a result of the frequent lead poisoning suffered by drinkers of stout from pewter tankards. A symptom of this malaise is a catatonic state resembling death, from which the sufferer may recover after a period of a few hours to a day or so, to the relief of those watching for signs of life.

The wake is an opportunity to celebrate the departed person's life in the company of his or her family and friends who will sit around drinking tea or whiskey, eating sandwiches and cake and chatting - often in the room where the body is laid out, and to mark the dead person's departure from their home for the last time.

For recent immigrants to America in the early part of the twentieth century, the wake was held in the dead person's home, in the typically old Irish fashion. There was very little sadness demonstrated, except by the close family, who were gathered around the coffin and attended by the priest most of the time. For the rest of the relatives and friends it was a party, a time to tell stories about the deceased and to air grievances.

CHAPTER SIX

The Wake

It was Friday and Daddy came home while we were eating supper. He tossed his cap on a chair and threw a packet across the kitchen table, almost knocking off one of the plates.

"And what is that?" Mama asked, lips tight, her voice quiet and harsh.

"That's the money you've been at me about, don't ye know." He sat down and looked at the vegetable soup and bread set out for the meal. "There's no meat here," he said. His large body was bent over the table, his black eyebrows trying to meet in protest.

"Meat! Is it meat you are wanting? You have the hell of a nerve coming in here with your little bit of money and expecting meat! Get it at the saloon! That's where you left the rest of your bit of money."

"Well, I'll just keep my money then and eat at Johnny's Place." He reached out for the small pile of bills, but Mama grabbed first and stuffed it in her apron pocket. "Oh, no you don't!" she growled at him. "You can tell those bums to feed you if you want meat!"

I was frightened. Why didn't Mama just leave him alone? All of us just sat still as if we were playing statues. Daddy picked up the plate and threw it on the floor. The crashing sound that it made acted like the bell that began the rounds in the boxing matches on the radio. Mama moved her body so that both feet were firmly on the floor; she dug her hands into her hips, her mouth became an even thinner line.

That's right!" she said, ignoring us children. "Break up everything! That way we'll have less to move when they put us out on the street!"

I could see it, the furniture piled up on the sidewalk, us sitting on the kitchen chairs. Mary would be in charge because

Mama would be working. Betty would put her thumb in her mouth and lean on Mary's knee, and Jackie would be gone, sneaking out through the back yard, climbing the fence to the alley.

Joe would toddle around, crying but charming. "Oh, you sweet baby," people would say. Margie would be asleep on my lap; she was little and charming, too, but nobody would notice. I could imagine the neighbors watching, the women clucking their tongues in sympathy. They would wrap blankets around us when it rained and ask in gentle tones where Mama was.

"You go to hell!" My father's voice wiped out the scene. He picked up his cap and was gone, slamming the front door with a final expression of anger. Mama stared at the door for a moment then turned back to us.

My stomach was heaving and I started to cry. "Will we really have to move because of Daddy?" I asked, trying to stifle the tears. I caught some with my tongue, trying to swallow the fear with the salty taste. I didn't want to hear the answer, I didn't want to hear what Mama might say.

"Eat your supper!" she commanded and moved about the kitchen making herself a cup of tea, the consolation for all miseries.

I never thought much about Margie and Joe, and sometimes forgot about them altogether. When Mama had a job cleaning at night at Montefiore Hospital Daddy took care of them a lot of the time. Joe was only three and Margie was going on four or maybe five. They were so quiet it was as if they were in a different family. I don't think they could cope with the rest of us unruly big kids. They both had straight hair while the rest of us had curly or wavy hair; Margie's was brown and Joe's was blond and they both had brown eyes like Daddy's.

Mama took the money and went shopping for groceries at the Economy store. The food was cheaper there. When we didn't have any money, Mary or I had to go to the corner store, Kuntz's, and get things on the bill. Mary never said much about it but I hated it. When I had to go I would stand outside the big window until the store was empty. Then I would walk in as fast as I could, give Mrs. Kuntz the list of groceries, and watch her write it all down on a small, thick white tablet that had carbon paper between the sheets so she would have a copy of it. She would stab her copy on a sharp spindle that stood near the cash register and hand me mine. She always smiled, but I couldn't smile back and rushed out of the store.

It was another week before Daddy came home again. I was not expecting him. We never knew how long he would be gone after one of those fights, but it was usually a longer time. I was sweeping the floor when I heard his shuffle, his feet dragging along the linoleum in the hall. He stopped at the kitchen door for a minute and inspected the room. Seeing me he nodded his head. "Mecushla," he said. He sometimes called me that, dear one or something like that in English, when he was a little bit drunk, just enough of the drink to feel nice. His shoulders were hunched under his jacket, his beard was shaggy and seemed to be all over his face. He took a can of chile con carne out of his pocket, pulled a chair from the table and set it near the stove, took a knife from the drawer in the little table between the windows and sat down to open the can, driving the knife into a top edge and pushing it in with his hand, then pulling it back until it made a slit in the top. He put some water into a cooking pot and set the can in it. The whole thing was so familiar that it would have been comforting except that just then Mama came into the kitchen.

"So ye're back are ye?" She slammed the bag of groceries onto the table and switched to the Irish. That was our cue to head for the third floor, our refuge from the storm of anger. We sat on our beds, waiting for the yelling to stop. A lump of sadness and fear settled into my chest. Margie and Joe fell asleep. Betty sucked hard on her thumb.

"I'm going to read," Jackie announced and swaggered over to his room, as if he didn't care.

"He got a comic book," Mary said. Mama didn't allow

us to read comic books but Jackie managed to get three cents for used ones somehow. "I wish I had a movie magazine," I said.

Finally it became quiet and Mama called. Daddy was sitting on the back porch eating from his can and Mama was putting the dishes on the table. "Eat your supper!" was her only comment. I looked around to see if Daddy had broken anything. He never hit Mama or any of us, but he worked for Uncle Pat for a while when he first got here from Ireland and one time broke up everything in Uncle Pat's saloon when he was drunk. Our cousin from Chicago told us that story and I never wanted to believe it, but every time he and Mama started fighting I thought of it.

I learned the family history through my habit of hiding under tables, and wakes were a good time to do that. The children were not spared the experience of going up to the casket, which before the days of funeral homes was set across two chairs in the living room. Nor were we spared saying a prayer while staring in horror or curiosity at the body. A three day wake was enough time to tell all about the life of the deceased with a lot of whiskey and laughter and stories. The kitchen was the gathering place for the men while the women stayed with the body and said their "Ora Mushas" and the rosary to help the poor soul get into heaven. A white tablecloth covered the big kitchen table and it was easy to sneak away from my mother and find a place by my father's knees. There was always some kernel of truth in the stories and if I heard the same one a few times I began to believe it, like I believed there was a greenhorn monster.

I thought of Uncle Paddy's wake. He was my mother's brother, had come over from Ireland not too long before he died of tuberculosis. The men talked about Uncle Paddy and what he did and recited the jokes he told them about the hospital the Public Health Department had shipped him off to. They went off on lots of other stories about Ireland: the way the ocean looked on a sunny day, the soft feeling of the mist when you could hear the whispering in the old cemetery on the edge of the sea; the waves dancing like they were tipped with jewels; the heavy sound the waves made when the wind was wildly throwing them against the rocks on the shore; the big light in the steeple of the church, The Star of the Sea, that was always lit as soon as the sun went down.

I heard about the poteen and how sometimes the young men would swim out from the mainland and buy some, drink too much and drown while trying to swim back across the bit of ocean to get home. They told some funny stories, too, and laughed out loud about them, like the one Uncle Paddy used to tell about Aunt Pegeen, my mother's sister, when she drank some of the poteen and danced over the rocks, singing and laughing and had to be rescued by one of the men.

Most of what I knew about my father I learned at those wakes. Daddy was an illegal immigrant and was granted amnesty after World War II. Sometime in the early 1900s Uncle Eddie joined the English navy, went to Canada, jumped ship and crossed the border to the United States. How my father got here with him was not explained but there were lots of stories about his adventures. Andd there were tales about his life in Ireland; nine children and their parents lived in a tiny cottage in Lettermullen, a village island connected to the mainland by a bridge.

"Ah, an O'Beara and a McDonagh never would have married in Ireland," said Uncle Eddie.

"Why not?" I had the temerity to ask the first time I heard it.

"Well" he said, "everybody over there wondered what kind of a wild family they would have over here. She to get on, and him to fight for the fun of it. And drink! The O'Bearas have to have their drinking. John O'Beara was never the one to hold his drink."

"And the McDonaghs made the poteen for them to drink." Uncle Pat said. "And them McDonaghs never associated with the O'Bearas." He twirled his cap, musing for awhile.

There were no tender stories about leprechauns or shamrocks, only the ocean and the fishing boats and the rocks and the carrying of the kelp to fertilize between the stones so the cows would have some grass to eat and the barley would grow for the making of the poteen. The stories were about the ones lost at sea, the disappearance of brothers and cousins in the storms. I imagined the fury of the wind as the families stood on the rocks and watched for the missing boats, the men quiet, the women crying loudly when one of the fishing boats did not return after a storm and the brothers and cousins were thrown up on the shore by the waves and recognized by the family pattern of their cable knit sweaters. "I knew one of them was gone," some wife or mother would say, "sure and I heard the wailing of the Banshee last night."

"It was a hard life," Uncle Eddie said, shaking his head from side to side. "And not much better here. Digging ditches is no better than hauling fish from the sea. And if you don't have the citizenship papers that's all you are going to do."

I could barely hear the women in the living room in quiet vigil around the corpse, saying the rosary, asking the Blessed Mother to guard the soul from the devil until he could enter heaven. There was no nostalgia for Ireland, no story telling and laughter in here. Talk turned to worries about unruly renters, husbands hiding in saloons spending the grocery money, and for God's sake, how were we going to pay the rent?

All of us children were left to wander around, eat the food and listen to the stories. It never occurred to me then that this was a ritual to mask the sorrows and trials of everyday life. I think the Irish truly believed that the corpse was only a symbol of the person who had gone to a place where he or she would be truly happy.

Riding the Rails in the 1930s

Many people during the depression heard about work hundreds of miles away - or even half a continent away. Often the only way they could get there was by hopping on freight trains - illegally. More than two million men and perhaps 8,000 women became hoboes, as they were called. At least 6,500 hoboes were killed in one year either in accidents or by railroad "bulls," brutal guards hired by the railroads to make sure the trains carried only paying customers. Finding food was a constant problem. They often begged for food at a local farmhouse. If the farmer was generous, the hobo would mark the lane so that later hoboes would know this was a good place to beg.

Riding the rails was dangerous. Most hoboes would hide along the tracks outside the yard. They would run along the train as it gained speed, grab hold and jump into open boxcars. Many lost their legs or their lives. As the train reached its destination a new set of "bulls" would arrest them or beat them up. But no

amount of clubbing or shooting could keep all
the hoboes off the trains. In many cases, they
had no other choice but to hop a freight and
look for work.

CHAPTER SEVEN

Christmas

Daddy was home for a long while. Mama was able to get enough sleep and go to work without being so tired and angry all the time. Daddy took Margie and Joe for walks, sang songs for them, talked to them and even played some card games with them. He sometimes played harder card games with Mary, Jackie, Betty and me after school. On Sundays Mama gave him twenty five cents, enough money to buy a street car pass and he took each of us in turn for a street car ride.

Street car riding was also a cultural event. There was no charge for visiting libraries, museums, parks, and the planetarium. I guess we were not very science oriented so the planetarium was usually the last on our list, even though it was the closest. But Daddy made the decisions, so we learned some things in spite of ourselves. In the center of the big lobby there was a huge brass pendulum hanging from the high ceiling. It swung slowly around the circumference of a circle circumscribed in the floor and it had numbers around the perimeter of the circle. I never did understand what it meant, only that it had something to do with measuring something about the world but I was transfixed by the slow, constant motion of the pendulum.

The Carnegie Museum and the Central Carnegie Library were in one long building in Oakland, about an hour's ride from home. Daddy seemed to like that the best and we went there often. He would sit in the reading room of the library while we, whoever of us kids he took with him for the day, would go to see the dinosaur skeletons dominating the central hall of the museum. I would walk around them and wonder, but there was nobody to explain anything about them, so they seemed like part of a fairy tale. Then I went to the next floor, past the Roman statues and the monstrous carved doors with barely a glance, to visit the wax Indians on the top floor.

The Indians were life size figures enclosed in a glass case; a woman wearing a sandy colored shawl bending over a triangle of sticks representing a small fire, stirring something in a pot; a man standing by wearing a feathered headdress, his arms folded on his chest over a shirt with colored beads adorning it; and a child sitting on the ground nearby. They were so lifelike that I wished that I could talk to them.

I considered the North Side library ours; we didn't need anybody to take us there. It was about a 20 minute walk from our house and Mary and I and sometimes Betty went to the story hour on Saturday mornings. We went down curved marble steps to the lower floor, sat on the steps while the librarian sat on a chair at the bottom of the steps and read fairy tales. Her words floated through the air creating visions of girls wearing filmy, beautiful dresses, handsome men dressed in silver armor and riding horses decked out in colorful blankets and fancy trimmings.

After the stories were over the others walked and I floated upstairs and found other kinds of books to take home for a week. That is if we didn't owe so much money for overdue books that we were restricted from borrowing any more. There were times when I was outlawed for months and suffered when I had to read Mary's kind of books, serious ones about real life problems, unlike mine which were romantic travel stories. She snuck into the adult book section, just like I did, and if the librarian didn't look too closely at us, we got books they thought we couldn't read.

Occasionally, when the weather was nice, Daddy would take one of us to the zoo. I was not impressed with anything there except the giraffes with their long, elegant necks and great, soft looking brown eyes that never blinked, I was terrified of the bears, they were too close for my comfort; there was only a short wall and a moat separating them from us. The whole place smelled pretty bad.

Mary got the most turns on the street car rides with Daddy. She loved to see the whole city and soon knew all of the routes by heart. I usually got motion sick so didn't want to go very often. Jackie would only go to the museum or the planetarium and Betty was too active, so Daddy took her to the North Side park where she would sit for long periods of time on the iron deer that looked blindly at the fence above the railroad tracks.

One Sunday, about two weeks before Christmas, we walked over the Sixth Street bridge toward downtown to see the Christmas store windows. There were four major department stores in Pittsburgh - Kaufmans, Hornes, Gimbels and Frank & Seder - located at various spots in the relatively small downtown area. After Thanksgiving every year each of these stores decorated several of their huge display windows with toys and animated figures and electric trains. The stores were closed on Sundays but crowds of people came into town to look at the windows.

Daddy was holding Betty's hand. "I don't see why she's going with us," I said. "She'll grab toys off the counter and the sales ladies won't let us look at them or touch them if she does that."

"It's Sunday," Mary said. "We're just going to look at the windows. Remember last year how they had the elves that were making toys in Santa's workshop?"

"Do they leave the windows running when the store is closed?" I asked.

"Well, sure," Mary said, fixing the collar of her coat, "all they have to do is leave the electricity on. That's what makes them move."

That's what makes them magical, I thought. I remembered about the windows; even when the figures didn't move, they were wonderful. Santa and the elves had happily smiling faces and wore red and green suits that fit tight on their legs and across Santa's big stomach. The dolls were all dressed in beautiful clothes, the baby dolls were in bassinettes with lace trim around the edges and bunches of white coverings; the little girls stood with their arms reaching out, their feet in shoes with

71

buckles, in dresses of lovely colors, hair curled and with bows to match the trim on the dress.

Betty was jumping on the sidewalk ahead of Daddy and then back again, grabbing his hand and making faces at Jackie, who was running a stick along the railing, making a steady clicking noise. When Daddy paid no attention to this, Jackie put his feet in the open part of the metal and pulled himself up so that he could lean over and spit in the river.

"Hey, quit it!" Mary yelled. "The wind's blowing your spit on my coat!"

Daddy didn't pay any attention until Jackie kicked a stone that hit Betty in the leg. She started screaming and Daddy picked her up, still ignoring Jackie. So he sulked until we got to the stores.

Even Betty was quiet as we slowly walked one block after another, staying longer in front of one that had a miniature train loaded with toys chugging across the front of the window, going through a tunnel and back again and again.

Daddy stood with Jackie and watched, letting Jackie slide his hand into his and Mary took Betty's.

"Did you ever ride on a train, Daddy?" Jackie asked after they had been watching for a while.

"Sure and I did." Daddy said no more for a few minutes and we waited. "That I did," he finally said again. "When these hard times started," he glanced at us, "I had no work and rode the rails for a time." Another pause. I held my breath. "See those cars with the doors on them?" he asked.

"Yes," we all agreed.

"Well, now, you could get those doors open when none of the railroad guards were watching and you could climb in there and sleep until the train came to another place. You never knew where that would be, or if one of those guards would open the doors and you might wind up in jail in some godforsaken town for a while." He chewed on the memory while people moved around us. "It was good for a while. We got food from the people in those towns; we built a fire near the train yard and sat around and talked the blarney and jumped on the next train that was going out of town." He started moving away from the window. "Ah well," he said.

The walk back was colder; the wind was blowing harder from the river, Daddy carried Betty and she fell asleep in his arms.

The next week Daddy was gone again and Christmas was only a week away. In the evenings Mama sat in her rocker smoking one of Daddy's corn cob pipes. The lump started in my chest again and I sat on the step and watched her until she gave a long sigh, put the pipe down and pushed herself out of the chair. She didn't knock the pipe on her other hand or blow through the stem like Daddy did when he finished smoking, she just left it on a table beside the chair he always sat in.

On the last day of school before Christmas some of the children were called out and went in a line to the school basement. Against one wall was stacked a pyramid of toys, dolls and trucks nestled next to each other in the large pile. I looked for a Shirley Temple doll, pushing aside some of the trucks and ordinary looking baby dolls.

"You will have to pick one," a gentle voiced Sister said. I took the first baby doll that was near me and followed the line back to the classroom, trying to hide the doll behind my back. I thought all of the children who had stayed in the classroom were watching me. I would have felt different if it was a Shirley Temple doll; I wouldn't have felt so embarrassed. I could see Priscilla snickering at me. Her family had money and she wore a pretty dress with a sash and a big ribbon in her hair. I hated her.

On Christmas Eve Mama put a red cellophane wreath in each of the two living room windows and left after supper. "I'm going out," she said, looking at me and Mary. "Put Margie and Joe to bed."

I took my favorite position on the steps in the hall after they were asleep. Mary and Jackie sat with me for a while. "What are you waiting for?' Jackie asked. "Mama doesn't have any money to get anything for us for Christmas." He stomped up the steps to his room, with Mary right behind him, never saying a word. I moved to be out of the light from the front room. I didn't know what I was waiting for, maybe for some miracle to happen so we would get some Christmas presents, or a push from God to send Daddy home, or just not to have Mama so sad.

I was half asleep when Mama came in carrying a bulging bag in each hand. She set them on the floor, locked the front door and hardly glancing at the steps, picked them up and went into the front room. The sliding doors were open all the way and I could see the couch under the windows. I watched as Mama opened one of the bags and pulled out a fire truck, set it in the middle of the couch and then place a smaller one beside it. She picked up a doll from the other bag and put it in the corner of the couch, smoothed the pink skirt, arranged the arms as if they were asking to be picked up. Two more little girl dolls went beside it with just as much care, one wearing a blue dress, the other a green. The blue one's for Betty, I thought; she loved blue. And Mary has green eyes so the pink one is mine. I wished it was Shirley Temple doll with red dots on the skirt.

A baby doll wearing a white bonnet trimmed in lace appeared last. A soft, cuddly one for Margie. Mama stood back to look at the toys, rearranged them, smoothed the skirts on the dolls again, placed the trucks just so. She sat down on the rocker and watched them and I watched her. The miracle had happened. Daddy wasn't coming home but Mama was smiling. I went up to bed and the lump in my stomach was gone.

The next morning we went to 9 o'clock mass. "Mama," Jackie asked in between spurts of jumping whole blocks of sidewalk, "Why do Margie and Joe have to come? They don't know anything."

"Never you mind, they have to learn sometime." Mama grabbed his arm. "And settle down. I don't want to see you carrying on in church."

The church had that little hum and rustling that happens when people are still coming in and finding seats. Mama led us right up to the first pew in front of the Blessed Mother's altar. It was covered with Christmas trees that smelled just like I imagined a pine forest would smell. Right in the center was the stable with no front but with hay scattered over the roof and all over the floor. There was the Blessed Mother in her blue cape over a white dress, kneeling and looking at the baby Jesus in the little hay filled bassinette. Saint Joseph was standing back a little, wearing his usual brown robe, holding a long staff and looking stern. There were sheep and a donkey standing around, too. The baby Jesus was wrapped with white cloth and he had his hands raised as if he were asking to be picked up. Lights high up in the ceiling shone down on them, the choir started to sing Christmas hymns. Margie let out a soft, "oooh!" It was like looking into the windows of the downtown stores, like Cinderella must have felt when she saw the magic coach.

Mrs. Absolutely

She was a little woman
birdlike in her twittering.
Lifting her umbrella
she pointed first at one
and then the other.
"Now you girls," she chirped,
"I saw you peeking into windows!
What would your mother say?"
We knew what our mother would say:
"Ora Musha! What am I going to do with you?"

The ladybird pursed her beak.
"I won't tell her this time but
if I see you again, I absolutely will.
Absolutely!"
Tapping the umbrella against her shoe
she left us politely waiting
until she turned the corner
head high, small feet clicking
on the slate sidewalk.

Then we twirled and laughed
with the joy of deceit.
"Oh, yes, Absolutely! Absolutely!
We will be good, Mrs. Absolutely!"
Absolutely!"

Shirley Temple Dolls

The twentieth century and it's multimedia created the current culture and cult of celebrity in which we live today. Shirley Temple is an early example of this cult. World famous from her movies, she was a merchandising dream. The highly prized original Shirley Temple dolls were produced between 1934 - 1939. Considering that TV wasn't available to promote mass market dolls when the Shirley Temple was released, the number of sales was a phenomenon.

The Shirley Temple dolls were made of a sawdust-based wood pulp composition that was later painted flesh-toned. She had hazel eyes with upper lashes of real hair, and painted eyebrows, lower lashes, lips and nostrils. Her wigs were made of mohair and styled in golden curls similar to Shirley's. Her clothes were copies of Shirley Temple's own clothes and the outfits that she wore in her extravagantly successful movies.

CHAPTER EIGHT

The Holes in the Wall

Charles Street started at a junction of three other streets that formed a wheel with four spokes. The center part was a wide oval space where cars could go through without benefit of traffic lights to slow them down. There were few cars at the time but I was always aware that one of them could find me. The street ended about a mile uphill at an intersection with another, more placid business area. Some of the houses had narrow alleys between two of them, a good place to hide when we played hide-and-seek if there was no locked gate at the front end. Our house was part of a row of about twenty houses with no space between. We had an enclosed back porch, a twin of the one next door, with only one wall of bricks between.

There were a lot of small depressions in the surface on the bricks of that wall. Daddy told us that they were bullet holes made by the bootleggers, men who made whiskey, violating liquor laws called prohibition, and lived in our house at one time. This seemed believable because one of Daddy's friends, whom he said was a gangster, got killed one night when he opened his front door and somebody shot him. Daddy said that he himself was not a bootlegger, although he tried making wine which exploded one night in his bedroom because he had hidden it behind the bedroom door and forgot about it.

The shooting made me fearful for a long time. Mr. Sable's daughter went to our school and I was sure that because Daddy knew Mr. Sable, and that Daddy must be in danger of the same thing happening to him. I had an almost permanent picture in my mind of him opening the door and falling to the floor in a puddle of blood. I worried constantly, and even asked Mama to tell him not to answer the door.

"Ora Musha," she said, "did ye ever see him answering the door, or be here when the doorbell rings?" And then, after some thought she added, "It would only be the man for the sweeper or the couch money or the insurance money, anyway." We would only open it for the insurance man, the only bill Mama ever paid when someone came collecting for a bill. She always paid the rent, too, but she went down to the corner and across to the Savings and Loan Association to pay that. This fear of answering the door has lasted a lifetime. I still have a need to know who is there before I open the front door of our house.

We knew the shooting was true because the story was in the daily paper, the Pittsburgh Press, and caused more commotion than news of a lady down the street winning the daily number. This number was based on the last three numbers of the stock market report and everybody on our street seemed to play their penny every day. For that penny you played the number straight, and got six dollars if you won. For four cents you could box the number. 'Boxing the number' was if you played the number 123 it would be played four different ways: 123, 132, 231 and 321. If any of those four numbers came out, you won your six dollars.

Ma Barnes, who lived across the street, sat on her front porch and collected the money, then delivered it to some place that we never knew. "The police station," Mama would mutter. Not that she cared. She played our house number, one way or another, every day and "never won a cent," she said. Maybe she was just being nice, she often took the penny over herself and stayed to talk to Ma Barnes for a while.

I liked Ma Barnes, too. She always said hello to whoever was passing by and sometimes sent her son, Pokchops, over to watch us when Mama was gone somewhere for a little while and Daddy wasn't home. Pokchops, I never knew him by any other name, was only fifteen or so, but when he lunged across the street his big shoulders would swing back and forth and he took giant steps just like Daddy did. He never said anything, just gave us a big grin as he sat down on the front step and prepared to keep an eye on us.

Betty and I sometimes checked the marks on the bricks on rainy, dull days. One day a coming storm made the porch dark and I noticed a pencil of light coming through an opening above the ice box. The box was a small one which held only twenty five pounds of ice, brought by an Italian man who carried it with big black tongs, like scissors with sharp ends holding the ice. I liked to watch him flip open the top, drop the ice with a crash, clamp the tongs so the points were together, slam down the lid and wave goodbye to us as he went back out through the kitchen. He and Mama laughed together before she gave him the dime for the ice.

By moving a chair next to the ice box, one of us could climb to the top of it. We took turns looking through the hole which gave us a view through the open door of the kitchen next door.

"Mrs. French is smoking a cigarette!" I said, turning to Betty.

"Let me see! Let me see!" Betty was jumping up and down eager to see this grand event. I moved back on the chair so she could look through the hole. "We should tell Mama," she said. "Maybe she could smoke a cigarette instead of Daddy's pipe."

We took turns watching, me thinking about the bad women in the gangster movies who lounged at the doorways of the speak-easys, (a name used for saloons hidden behind guarded doors), wearing satin, slinky gowns, watching gunmen plan their moves. Maybe a bullet had gone through one of those holes and killed somebody. After all, maybe Daddy's story was true and that was why Mr. and Mrs. French never came out to sit on the front steps the way most of the other neighbors did. I began to feel guilty watching. Cherie French, who was in my room at school, lived there and I felt like I was spying on her. They must have had more people living in their house than we did in ours because Cherie and her brother slept on the porch.

We were watching the progress of the burning cigarette when Betty slipped and fell to the floor and Mama made her entrance. "Oeeyauld!" she yelled at me. The Irish word meant that she was mad but not enough to do anything about it at the moment. She didn't ask what we were doing so we never gave her the suggestion about the cigarettes.

Later, after the dishes were done and we had washed our underwear for the next day, Mary and I talked about Cherie's father.

"I guess her mother is sad," Mary said. "He doesn't have a job, either."

"How do you know?" I asked.

"I know," she raised her head and tried to look down her nose at me, "because I heard Mrs. Morrow tell some lady at the store that he is an engineer and even he can't get work. You know what she said?"

"What?" I thought he had a job. Mama said he was very educated.

"She said they were too proud to go on welfare and she didn't know what they were living on."

"They must be poorer than us," I said. I thought about that for a while. "But then, how come Cherie got a Shirley Temple doll for Christmas?" The doll was just like Shirley; she had curly hair, a firm body, arms and legs that you could move back and forth and was dressed in an outfit from one of her movies, usually a white dress with red polka dots. A little red ribbon was attached to her hand; when you moved the arm up it stayed there and held the skirt of the dress just like the real Shirley did. She looked she was just about to curtsy. The doll I got for Christmas was not as pretty. She was bald with hair molded on; you had to run your handover the top of her head to feel it. The arms and legs were attached to a body made out of white cloth that turned gray almost immediately. It was stuffed with something that got lumpy when you held it too hard. The fingers on the hand were stuck together, not separated like Shirley's. It didn't have a name either. But it was soft and nice to hold. And I loved it because Mama got it for me. Even so, I still longed for one of those Shirley Temple dolls. I think if somebody gave me one now, seventy some years later, I would be almost as thrilled.

It seemed like there were always a lot of people living in our house. So we lived at various times on various floors of the house, depending on what floor Mama was renting out. This always happened on May 1, Moving Day.

"There's no law that says you have to move that day," Mary told me. "Daddy said that people just started moving then and it became a habit because everybody knew you could find a place that somebody moved out of."

That Moving Day Mary, Jackie and I were watching Mama. We were sitting on Cherie's step, having been told to stay out of the way while mama put furniture out on the sidewalk. It belonged to the people upstairs in our house and they had refused to move.

"You old witch! What do you think you're doing?" Mrs. Angelino screamed so loudly that everybody in the neighborhood heard it. I saw heads popping out doors and kids running up the street to see what was happening. We were embarrassed by Mama's actions and afraid of Mrs. Angelino's anger.

"What do you think I'm doing?" Mama yelled back, her soft brogue gone, her voice sounding angry and harsh. I think she was embarrassed, too. She never sounded like that except when she got really mad at Daddy when he was drunk. "You don't pay the rent, you get out!" she said. She was carrying two chairs and set them down on the sidewalk in front of the house. The chairs were nicer than any of ours; the legs were carved out of dark, shiny wood and the seats and backs were covered with dark red velvet.

Mama pulled a paper out of her apron pocket and waved it in front of Mrs. Angelo's face. "You see this?" Her voice was a little softer. "This paper is from the police. See here?" She stabbed at the paper with her finger. "This tells me I can put your furniture out on the sidewalk for not paying rent for three months."

Mrs. Angelino hardly glanced at the paper. She pushed it aside and let out a lot of Italian words. "I bet she's swearing in Italian," I said.

"I bet she's saying Mama wrote that paper herself," Jackie said.

"Oh," I said. "Did she?" Mama wouldn't do something like that, I thought. That would be a lie and she would never lie. She did say some words in Irish, though, that I knew were swear words, then she said in English: "There's lots of places you can go."

I could see some other houses had furniture piled up on their sidewalks, too. "Maybe Mr. and Mrs. Angelino can rent in one of those houses," I said. I liked the Angelinos. They were nice to us, never told us we were stomping up and down the steps, and had given us candy at Halloween. They kept the bathroom clean, too, so I never had to do it.

"Nah," said Jackie, "who would rent to somebody if they know they don't pay their rent." He jumped to his feet. "I'm leaving," he said.

"Oh, no you don't!" Mama heard him. "You get up there and help your father take that bed apart and bring it down." She didn't tell me and Mary to do anything, so he made a face at us. It didn't mean anything, he liked to help Daddy.

I thought the Irish were the only ones who didn't pay their rent. Mama had to get some of them out the year before but there wasn't any screaming, just a few Ora Mushas and Oeeyaulds and some other Irish curse sounding words. They took their own furniture, too. And carried it away with them, a few pieces at a time, and disappeared around the corner at the top of the street.

"If we have to have rent money I wonder who will move into our house then." Mary and I stayed on the step contemplating the next move. "I know," Mary said. "Mama told me. The Nees. Mama said they're good people and weren't thrown out of their last house. Besides they're relatives."

"So why are they moving?" I asked.

"I don't know. Maybe they want to live with relatives. Mama said there's so many of them they can have the downstairs. She said she doesn't want them making all that noise over her head, and they'll pay more money because it's the first floor."

"Maybe they were too noisy." I hated the thought of moving up from the first floor. We never used the big front room and hardly ever the middle room, only in the winter when we dressed around the coal stove. But not having the kitchen! It was big and bright and we spent all our time there, especially in the winter. The upstairs kitchen was in the middle room. It had a big window and wasn't as dark as the middle room downstairs, but it was smaller and there was no porch. What would Daddy do without a porch to sit on and read his paper? And I was mad because Mama told Mary about the new renters and not me. I felt sad, too. I wished the Angelinos had paid their rent.

The nice thing about the move was that we were not so far away from Mama and Daddy. Joe had a bed in Mama and Daddy's room but the rest of us slept on the third floor, a long, long distance from the first. The four of us girls had the front room, larger than Jackie's room but so crowded with three beds that there was no room for anything else. A wide window sill made a good seat to look out and see the top of the street car when it went by, the electric line spitting little gold sparks. We could see more sky up there, too, but the windows were tiny so we couldn't see anything else. We complained for a long time about not being able to read up there.

"You can talk to each other," Mama said. "You do enough of it when you're not supposed to."

So we continued our ritual of telling dresses, which Mary did even in the daytime; she loved clothes so much. In fact, she loved them so much that when the Waldrons, one of our renters, set their mattress on fire and Mama called the fire department, Mary ran back up the steps when we were already halfway down, to get her clothes from the closet in the bedroom. Betty and I stood where she left us and screamed at her; we were afraid she would not be able to get out. We grabbed her and pulled her with us when she came through the little bit of smoke that was streaming up the steps. She must have had something new in the closet to have been so determined to get the clothes to safety. I couldn't think of any clothes of mine that would have made me do that.

For a while after that we talked about the fire, about Mama telling the Waldrons to get out, then the Angelinos moving because we needed the rent, and about the nice, handsome firemen who had raced up the steps and threw the burning mattress out the window.

Gangster Films of the 1930s

Gangsters of the early 1930s are characterized by their normality, and this essential normality is closely related to the ways in which fictionalizations of the gangster's career can act as wide-ranging critiques of American society and economic structures. A high-profile gangster, like any man trying to live with a public identity, poses the question of what drives such a man to succeed and what characteristics ultimately undermine his power.

Sharing an identity with respectable, law-abiding citizens but at the same time functioning outside the law, the gangster defies an unjust system. He both collides with and replicates this society's legitimate structures. Gangsters became symbols of a rebellion impossible for ordinary law-abiding citizens to enact. And this heroic rebel image was reinforced by Hollywood versions of the myth, featuring performances of great verve and energy.

Movie gangsters such as James Cagney, and Edward G. Robinson were heroes of dynamic gesture, strutting, snarling and posturing, possessing a blatant, anarchic appeal. Outside the law in a period when

Depression America was cynical about all sources of moral authority, they possessed an awe-inspiring grandeur, even in death. The criminal big-shot, viewed in the distorting mirror of the satirist, is a parody of the American dream of success. The inevitable fall of the big-time gangster is that of the victim of a society in which everyone is corrupt.

CHAPTER NINE

The Hypocrite

I was watching Betty coloring a picture of a dress I had drawn for her. She was kneeling on a chair, toes of her shoes stuck through the round slats in the back, her tongue locked between her teeth, helping her to weigh down the crayon.

"That dress looks funny," I said. "Why don't you color just the dress instead of scribbling all around it, too?"

"Because I'm going to cut it out," she said, frowning as she looked at it. "I saw the lazy Irishman" she added, stabbing the paper with a black crayon.

"What do you mean?" Mary asked.

"I did! I really did! You can ask Daddy!" Betty said.

"How would he know?" I asked.

"Because," she said, "when me and Daddy went for the street car ride on Sunday we saw Delia walking over the sixth street bridge with him and Daddy said "Well, there's Delia's Irish boyo." Betty scribbled some more, this time covering the dress. "I asked him if that was the lazy Irishman and he said that was him." She crumpled up the paper and threw it across the table. "Where do you find an Irish boyo?" she asked Mary.

"I think maybe at the Irish dances," Mary said. "They have them every week at the church. What did he look like?"

"Umm" Betty now had her hand under her chin, looking at us as if deciding whether to tell us any more. Mary scowled at her. "Tell us!" she demanded.

"Umm....well, he sort of looked like Daddy, but skinny." If Mary told Betty to do something, she did it.

We found out soon enough about him the next Sunday when Mama had Delia and the boyo for dinner I don't know why she did that; she never had people for dinner. People would visit and sometimes eat with us, but that was only uncles and aunts. I didn't like Ian and liked him even less that day. He was handsome, I guess, but not really. I don't know what I mean, but I think it's the way he looked at me, like one of those villains in the gangster movies that smile all the time and nobody knows why they're smiling. And he would talk to me and not to Mary and she was much better at talking than I was.

He was tall like Daddy and had black hair, but his eyes were blue, not a mixed up blue like mine, but clear with no little specks in them. He smiled at me when Delia told him my name and said: "Well, you're a pretty little one." Delia poked him with her elbow. "Aunt Bridgie wouldn't like to hear you saying that." I didn't like it either. He laughed, hardly opening his mouth and I thought maybe he was hiding ugly teeth.

"Smarmy, that's what he is!" Mama said. Calling him that may have been a suspicion that he was being too friendly, maybe something warning her that I was to beware of him. But talking about sex in any way was foreign to all of us. I didn't even know what it meant and probably Mary didn't either, not that I would have asked her. Mama frowned at me for a minute as if I had done something wrong. "Handsome is as handsome does," she muttered. I didn't know what it meant, and that sideways look kept me from asking. It was too bad that she didn't remember that when she sent me to baby sit for them later. I wished that she would have told me to stay away from him.

On Sundays we had our supper at lunchtime. It was a nicer meal than we had at other times. Mama was not tired, Daddy might be home, like he was today, and everybody was still feeling good from church, except Daddy who hardly ever went to Mass. We had enough meat for everybody to have a big piece, not like during the week when sometimes we only got a little bit, if any. We always had dessert, too; pies when we had apples, bread pudding with lots of raisins when we didn't. And mashed potatoes. This was the only time when Mama would mash them instead of putting them on the table with their skins on and we burned our fingers peeling them.

Delia was wearing a dress that was yellow with flowers

on it, not tiny ones like on the dresses Mama and the neighbors wore, but big ones of different colors. It had a collar that floated across her shoulders in a wave and came down over her arms instead of a sleeve. The skirt was wavy, too, and flared out at the bottom. Even Daddy noticed it and said: "My, that's a grand looking dress you're wearing, Delia." She must have been as surprised as I was because she didn't say a word, just looked at him. I was thinking Delia shouldn't wear yellow, it didn't go with her freckled face and wrinkly red hair.

But Ian had some words to say. "Isn't she the darling, now?" he said. "I talked her into getting it. I'm thinking she can wear it on her honeymoon." He smoothed back his hair, as well as his voice, smiled and looked around the table.

Mama dropped her fork just when she was going to take a big bite of chicken, and even Daddy put his fork down. "And what's this about a honeymoon, Delia?" Mama asked. "Are you planning to get married, then?"

That's what I wanted to talk to you about, Aunt Bridgie," Delia said. "I'm wondering if we could have the wedding from here?" Her voice was low and shaky. I was holding my breath and thought everybody else was, too, they were all so quiet.

"From here? Glory be to God, and how would we do that? We haven't got two cents to rub against each other ourselves."

"But Ian has a job, Aunt Bridgie," Delia said. "He is a policeman at Westinghouse!"

"That's right," Ian said. "You wouldn't have to pay a thing."

"Ora musha! Not pay a thing, he says! If ever the time comes that I don't have to pay a thing I will be somewhere with the angels singing songs and having a glorious time. Not pay a thing, indeed!" Mama pushed her chair away from the table, grabbed the pot of potatoes from the stove and scooped them into the bowl on the table, banging the spoon against the pot and hitting the side of the bowl with each spoonful. "I'll say no more," she said. "We'll talk about it later."

"It's true, Aunt Bridgie," Ian said. I thought Mama would hit him with the spoon if he called her Aunt Bridgie once more and yell at him that I'm not your aunt and keep your smarmy words to yourself. But all she said was "Hmmpf!" Mary and I looked at each other. We hoped she would have the wedding. And she did.

Delia stayed at our house for two weeks before the wedding, mooning around again, looking at her face in the mirror, rushing in and out, coming home and telling us all about the beautiful dress she would wear.

"The doctor fired her," Mama said when I asked why she was around so much.

"Do you think she was really fired?" I asked Mary later.

"Maybe Mama is just saying that because Delia never gave her any money as long as she was working." I thought about that for a while. "I bet Delia quit so Mama wouldn't ask her for the money." I said, "And I bet Ian paid for the dress."

Delia's dress arrived the day before the wedding in a big box that Betty, Jackie and I took after the wedding for sliding down the hall steps. It was almost as good as rolling over and over down the long, grassy hill in the park. When I saw the bridal dress on Delia I forgot that this was the bushy haired greenhorn that invaded our house a year before. She looked like she was in a Joan Crawford movie. The dress was white satin with a small train that just touched the floor in back and showed her white satin shoes in front. It had a sweetheart neckline, I guess because the neckline was shaped like a heart in front and long sleeves that came to a point on the back of her hand. She wore a big creamy colored straw hat with a wide brim that dipped in the front and had a huge white flower on one side. She touched the banister with her right hand and held a bouquet of blue flowers wrapped in satin ribbon in the other. She didn't look at all like Delia; she looked thinner and was smiling and looking around as if she were a princess.

I was glad I got to see the preview because I don't remember going to the wedding, so I guess Daddy must not have been around and I had to stay home and watch Betty, Margie and Joe. Or maybe Mary didn't go, either. I asked Mary recently if she remembered it and she didn't. When I think about it now, maybe none of us went. Maybe Daddy was gone again, or still. I think that happened so often and made me so sad that I shoved all the leavings and returns to the back of my mind and forgot them.

We didn't see much of Delia after that. No more greenhorns came over, either; there was no opportunity for jobs. Sometimes I still went with Mama to visit Uncle Mike in East Pittsburgh, and past those rows of tall smokestacks in the neighborhoods along the river. Mama always said: "There's no smoke and no jobs," and that phrase has stayed with me, long past that time when the mills were not working and everything went down with them.

Later on, Mama would say that Delia didn't know what it meant to be poor. Ian always had the job at Westinghouse, which was not a mill but made train rails, and even though work was slow they were never completely shut down. When we passed the Westinghouse on our way to Uncle Mike's house it always reminded her of Delia.

"She has all that money now." Mama would say, "She could pay back some of it after all I did for her." Then she would go on to Ian's lack of gratitude. "And him! What can you expect from him? Smarmy, that's what he is." Sometime later when I learned what that word meant, I knew she was right. He was a hypocrite.

The Galway Hooker

In the time before trains and cars, transportation was a much more difficult affair. The quickest route for news, goods, or people was often by water. Hence Galway, on the west coast of Ireland, like any other port town, drew its wealth from the sea; both from fishing and from the extensive trade it carried on with France, Spain, and the West Indies.

One of the greatest actors to take the stage in this maritime adventure was the Galway Hooker. The Hooker was like no other craft, and its clever design was fitted purposely for the subtleties of Galway's waters. The term Hooker is known to apply to hook and line fishing. The boats are noted for their strong sharp bow and sides that curve outward like "the breastbone of a water fowl." The design, built largely of oak, was sturdy, stable and quick, allowing fishermen to navigate difficult passages, while hauling their cargo weighing upwards of twelve to fifteen tons.

The Hookers had their greatest presence in Galway Bay in the years preceding the Great Famine of the mid 1880s. Sadly, famine, depleted fishing stocks, and the advent of modern technology would eventually seal the Hooker's fate as a working vessel. She is still seen at Irish maritime celebrations such as The Gathering of the Boats.

CHAPTER TEN

The Boat in the Cellar

The boat in the cellar was a great mystery to us. It had been on an old work table for as long as I could remember. Whenever I asked Mama about it, she only said: "It's your father's. Now, ask me no questions and I'll tell you no lies." My cousin Eddie told me at a much later time that the boat was called a Galway Hooker, a fishing boat.

The boat was as long as my arms stretched out to both sides. The front was round and the sides curved until they met at a point in the back; the outside was painted with shiny brown paint that made it glow in the dim light. The inside was divided into sections with pieces of new wood curving from one side to the other. A tall piece, as thin as a pencil, supported a sail cut from cloth held at both ends with string attached to tiny metal circles. There was a railing all around it with little posts to hold it to the boat. It was as if some fairy came in during the night and added some delicate railings or a small set of sails held together with fine string, and a tiny pulley that only a small hand could carve. This was easy to believe, because none of us had ever seen Daddy working on the boat.

It had been a bad day at school. Our class was practicing for First Communion Day, a big event that was to happen some Sunday soon. Sister smacked my hand for talking when I was only listening to another girl telling me about her first communion prayer book. I didn't even want to hear it because the little book had a shiny cover like white patent leather shoes; when she opened it there was a gold carving of a crucifix in a nice little nest inside the cover. My communion prayer book was a dirty looking white with tiny pebbles covering it and not even pictures, let alone a gold cross.

Mama had gone to the store with Margie and Joe, and Mary and Betty had gone somewhere, so Jackie and I were home alone. He was heading for the back porch, the launch of his route over the back fence to find his friends. There was no gate in the back fence because the pickle factory in back of our yard came almost to the end of the fence.

"Come down to the cellar with me to look at the boat, please Jackie?" I asked. "I saw a big rat the last time I was down there." He gave me that superior look he had been using lately. He was a year older than me and Mama never made him stay home like she did us girls.

"Please?" I begged.

"Yeah? I bet you never saw a rat." He spoke out of the side of his mouth like Edward G. Robinson did in the movies. "A big rat could never fit in that sewer."

"I bet you never saw one. You're jealous," I said.

"Oh, yeah? Well, I bet I could kill this one if I saw him!" He flipped the light beside the cellar door. I held on to his shirt as we crept down the narrow stairs. The two small front windows were at pavement level, black with coal dust and gave little light. There was a dim light bulb dangling at the end of an electric cord in the center of the room. "I wonder how Daddy can even see to work on the boat down here," Jackie whispered.

He clutched my arm, peered over the shaky wood stair railing. "I bet that rat won't even come out again," he said. I bet Jackie's as scared as I am, I thought.

"Well," I said, "Mama said the rat won't come back now that the cat had her kittens."

A little cupboard on one side of the dresser in the dining room had been left open and the cat had laid the kittens there when they were being born. When we looked at them in the morning they were all slimy and so tiny they looked like little mice. The cat licked them while we were at school and the next time we saw them they were dry and crawling all over their mother to get their milk. The day after that their eyes were still closed but we tried to pet them and all we did was spill the milk Mama had put in the cupboard for the mother cat.

Cats were not a luxury in the 1930s. Cats came to your house because there were mice or rats somewhere around for food. The cats all looked the same, dark and light grey striped, with yellow eyes, and we called all of them "Kitty." They never stayed where they could be seen, except when they had babies to take care of. I never knew why they came to our house. Maybe Mama fed them at night or something. She must have liked them but could not afford to feed them. Besides, they probably wouldn't take care of the rats if she did.

The next day the kittens were gone and the cat would be hungry. Nobody said anything, but other times we had seen Daddy going down to the river with a bag wriggling in his hand and coming back with his hands in his pockets. It was a sad feeling. After all these years I can still bring the image to my mind of those tiny creatures, their wet, shiny fur clinging to their bodies, eyes tightly closed, huddled around the mother, whose eyes glared at me if I made a move to touch them. I wanted to pick them up and touch their fur when it dried and hold them like I would a doll. Like many other longings in my life, I remember it so well because it never came about.

Holding on to my shoulder, Jackie led me past the sewer, both of us looking only at the boat. It was still on its stand, the small knife, the pieces of string, the shavings from the wood had not been moved. "I knew Daddy wouldn't be here," Jackie sounded disgusted. "Why'd you drag me down here?"

"I just wanted to see if the fairies came," I said. I felt like crying now; first I got smacked, now Jackie was mad at me. He picked up one of the wood shavings, ran his fingers over it, then threw it back on the table. "Quit sniffling," he said. "that's little kid stuff. C'mon, let's go upstairs. I'm going out."

"Why doesn't Daddy work on the boat?" I asked Mama the next day.

"He works on it all right," she said, "when he gets a little bit of the whiskey in him and starts singing Irish songs." She was sitting in front of the stove in the kitchen holding Joe after giving him a bath in the big round wash tub. "Your father and his father before him used to make the fishing boats in Ireland. That was always their family's job. They went to school beyond anybody else and could measure and build them better than anybody in Galway." Her hands were still on Joe's back, holding the towel around him. Her eyes were not on him but on something I couldn't see; her voice sounded soft. "He was the best looking boy on the big island, he was. It was shocking to see him. That black hair and those brown eyes. Not many had that kind of eyes."

Mary, Jackie and I were sitting on the front steps watching the shadows of the houses across the street creeping over to the curb on our side. If they got much longer it would be too late to go down to the river.

"You ask Daddy," I said to Jackie. "Maybe he'll go down now."

"No, he won't do it for me." He kept rubbing a peach stone against the cement. If he rubbed long enough it would make a hole and make a whistling sound when you blew into it.

"You know he won't," he said. "You ask him, he likes you." He pushed the stone so fiercely that it split in half.

"See what you made me do?" He picked up the pieces, stood up, swung his arm over his head and threw them so hard that they bounced along the stone blocks between the street car tracks. "I hope the street car smashes them up," he said.

"What are you so mad about?" Mary asked. "Daddy likes all of us."

"I always have to go to the saloon and look for him and ask for money and he won't come home with me." Jackie sat on the step, crossed his leg over his knee and started to peel some rubber off the sole of his shoe. "Look at this! The dumb sole that Daddy put on last week is coming off already," he said as he pulled off another piece.

"You're going to pull it off all the way back to the hole," I told him. When we got holes in our shoes Daddy scraped the leather with a little metal scraper from a package with two pieces of rubber shaped to fit the bottom of the shoes. He put the shoe on a shoe last, an iron foot left in our cellar by one of the careless fairies, he said. He spread some of the glue that came with it onto the rubber, slapped it on the old sole and hammered on it so it would stick.

"If you walk down to the river you better put some more glue on it," I said.

Jackie got up and stomped his foot. "I don't need to glue it." He stomped some more and sat down again. "You go in and ask him, Anna," he said.

"You go," I said to Mary, "you're the oldest."

"That's what you always say when you don't want to do something." Mary gave me that Mama look that meant I didn't have any choice. Maybe Daddy did like me best. He didn't get mad at me the way he did with Jackie and sometimes with Mary. So I went and found Daddy on the back porch, drinking tea from a small cooking pot, holding it by the handles and taking big gulps of it.

"Why do you drink tea?" A silly question, everybody drank tea, but I didn't want to come right out and ask him to take us to the beach before it got dark. He set the pot on the floor and looked up at me.

"Because, Mecushla, it evens up the body temperature, you see." He called me Mecushla when he was feeling good. Mama would have said he had a little drink in him, that's why he was happy.

"Is it even enough to go to the river?" He smiled at my question. "Well, now, you may have a little bit of the old sod in you, too. Yes, it may be a grand day for the river." Then I felt good and wondered about tea and whiskey and why they made Daddy feel that way when just his words made me feel happy.

After I told Mama that we were leaving, Mary and I sat on the steps again and watched Jackie hitting the house with a small ball. He held it in one hand, patted it with the other, raised his arm over his head and looked intently at the wall.

"Watch that brick in the middle," he called out to us. "that's the one I'll hit."

"Showoff!!" I said. All the bricks looked alike to me.

We started down the street, Daddy taking his giant

steps, Jackie with his head down, kicking whatever he saw on the sidewalk. Our street ended where four others came together with it. In the center of all these streets there was an island of buildings, one of which was the Building and Loan where Mama went every week to pay our rent and came back angry and talking about the damn-bank and the damn-politicians who took our house away from us and made us pay to live there. This was another of those puzzles which always got the same answer: "Ask me no questions and I'll tell you no lies."

We crossed over all the streets, past the Brighton show. I wanted Daddy to stop long enough to see the new movie posters on the wall but he never even glanced that way. Jackie ran ahead and soon we heard a yell from him: "Look! Look! Daddy! There's a train going into the roundhouse!" He was standing on the crosspiece of an iron fence, his face scrunched against the opening between the uprights.

Daddy stopped right beside Jackie, put his hands in his pockets, pushed his cap back on his head and put one foot on the crosspiece. We watched the train slowly move along the track on the far side of the railroad yard, big bursts of white smoke spurting out of the engine. It crept into the dark cave of the roundhouse, its headlamp lighting up pieces of the wooden walls as it traveled the circle and came out heading in the other direction.

"See that now," Daddy said. "Where's that train going?" Jackie asked, moving closer to him.

"Maybe to Chicago," Daddy answered. "They bring the iron ore from there and have to go back for more for the steel mills." The smoke became little puffs as the train picked up speed. We watched until it was gone and the yard had become silent.

"Well, now. We better be off," Daddy said. Jackie moved with him and tried to match his steps. The sidewalks ended and we were walking on a dirt road. Jackie could not resist the chance to kick up dirt balls and raised a big cloud of dust so we almost missed the dusty pump in the middle of the road. Jackie grabbed the long handle and was trying to push it down far enough to bring the water. He was almost dancing in the air when Daddy came over, held one hand over Jackie's, and gave a strong push with the other. The water came bursting out, forcing us to jump out of the way.

"There, now," Daddy said, "get your drink." We took turns filling the cup that hung by a string from the pump, letting the water overflow on our hands before drinking out of it.

I could smell the river before I could see it. Mama always complained about that smell when we crossed the bridge going over town, but I liked it. It was like walking into the house and smelling bread that had just finished baking, knowing that I could have a piece of it while it was still warm. We ran to the edge of the water, took our shoes off and let our feet sink into the soft mud. Daddy stayed on the wooden benches further back near the trees where some other men were sitting.

The river water was a light brown color that moved around patches of green. When the sun was shining on some places it almost looked like gold. A long train of coal barges came by, pushed by a small boat, breaking up the gold into black and brown speckles.

"How could that little boat push all those barges?" wondered Jackie. "I'm going to ask Daddy." He jumped up, put his shoes on and ran toward the bleachers.

The water was beginning to turn all black at the other shore when Daddy came to get us. He was by himself. "Where's Jackie?" I asked with sudden fear. "He went up to talk to you."

"Sure, I didn't see him come up there," he said. "Would he have come when I was going for a little walk?" He turned away without waiting for an answer. He started taking huge steps, his shoulders hunched, his hands moving back and forth as he walked. He was going so fast that Mary and I had to run to keep up with him.

"Stay here," he said when we got to the bleachers and Jackie was nowhere to be seen. I held Mary's hand. The feeling inside me was worse that the one I got when Mama and Daddy kept yelling at each other and Daddy stomped out of the house. It seemed like the whole night went by before he came back but it didn't because there was still light in the back of the sky. It was behind him when he came around the end of the bleachers carrying Jackie, making his shadow reach us before we saw him.

Jackie was crying, his arms around Daddy's neck. "I was looking for you, Daddy, and I couldn't find you. I can never find you."

A Good Catholic Confession and The Family Rosary

The basic requirement for a good confession is to have the intention of returning to God like the 'prodigal son' and to acknowledge sin with true sorrow before the priest.

As a result of Original Sin, human nature is weakened. Baptism, by imparting the life of Christ's grace, takes away Original Sin and turns us back toward God. The consequences of this weakness and the inclination to evil persist, thus we often commit personal or 'actual' sin. There are two kinds of actual sin, mortal and venial.

Mortal sin is a deadly offense against God, so horrible that it destroys the life of grace in the soul. Three simultaneous conditions must be fulfilled for a mortal sin: 1) the act must be something very serious; 2) the person must have sufficient understanding of what is being done; 3) the person must have sufficient freedom of the will.

Which sort of free will is a question

that philosophers have debated for over two millennia. Much of the debate about free will centers around whether we human beings have it at all.

The essential sacrament of Penance, or Confession, is contrition; a clear and decisive rejection of the sin committed, together with a resolution not to commit it again because of the love one has for God, which is reborn with each repentance. The resolution to avoid committing these sins in the future is a sure sign that the sorrow is authentic, and the condition for forgiveness.

The Rosary is the essence of Catholic devotion in which vocal and mental prayer unite the whole person in effective and purposeful meditation on the central mysteries of Christian belief.

As a prayer for peace, the rosary has always been particularly effective as a prayer which brings the family together. Individual family members, in turning their eyes toward Jesus, also regain the ability to look one another in the eye, to communicate, to show solidarity, to forgive one another and to see their covenant of love renewed in the spirit of God.

CHAPTER ELEVEN

Learning to Lie

Mama and I were on our way to six o'clock mass, going through the park alone so early in the morning that the sky was still dark. The trees had strange shapes, going all the way up into blackness until their leaves disappeared. Even the birds that I heard in the daytime were quiet. I felt like I had to walk on tiptoe so I wouldn't wake them up. Mama must have felt that way, too, because she walked slower and didn't rock side to side like she does when she is in a hurry. I guess that's why she had to get new heels on her shoes so often; they got rundown on the outside edges.

She was wearing her church dress, a dark blue silky one with little white flowers on it, and a straw hat tilted on the side of her head. My dress was supposed to be my good one but seemed pretty old to me; Mary even wore it to school before I got it. I asked Mama once why she went to the early mass when she had a nice dress and could go to a later one when everybody wore good clothes. All I got in answer was a look.

A train whistle came from the other end of the park. As if it was a signal, the sky began to wake up at the same time that a bright light came around the bend.

"Let's watch the train!" I said, pulling Mama toward the black iron fence guarding the tracks. We watched the train roar past us, under the bridge and out of sight as fast as it had appeared, so sudden it was as strange as the dark tree shapes.

We went back to the path, around the little lake where the flat bottomed boats were, oars standing in a long row against the boathouse waiting for the daytime. The new light was brightening up the old brass cannon leaning against the brick wall of the rose garden.

"The roses must be opening up," I said. "I can smell them. I never smelled them out here before." Mama stopped, looking toward the wall, then up at leaves beginning to reflect the light. "Well," she said, "that may be. Your father would say it's a soft day." I couldn't remember ever feeling so happy with my mother.

The church was almost as dark as the outside, only a few of the lights were on in the distant ceiling. Rows of small candles flickered near the altar, tiny flames dancing in the little red glasses. People, mostly women, were scattered around the church, one or two to a pew. I could hear the hum of their voices, saying their rosaries in loud whispers.

We sat near the picture of The Mother of Perpetual Help, Mama's favorite image after the Blessed Mother statue. The statue stood in a niche on a side altar; she was wearing a blue cape and smiling at us. Inside the church was almost as lovely as the walk in the park. The colors in the high stained glass windows began to appear as the light moved along them, like God made the world, one piece at a time. I moved closer to Mama; I liked to touch that dress, it felt so soft and silky. I watched the priest move about the altar, his white and gold vestments glittering when the light touched it.

Mama and the other women kept right on praying their rosaries after the mass started. It didn't matter, the priest prayed in such a low voice that I could hardly hear him anyway and I guessed others didn't understand him any more than I did. One time I asked Daddy why the mass was said in Latin and he said: "God alone knows. Maybe they don't know any Irish."

"Did they say the Mass in Irish in Ireland?" I asked. "Well, now," he said, "we were not allowed to talk the Irish in Ireland, except when none of them nobs were around to hear us." I knew about that. Uncle Pat told us once that they had Irish school behind the rocks and bushes so the people who were in charge of Ireland didn't know they were speaking the Irish.

I wondered now what Mama was praying for. Maybe for Howie and Freddie, the boys across the street who died from diphtheria. There had been a yellow sign beside their front door for about a week with big black letters saying the house was quarantined. One day it was gone and they were gone and after that their mother never sat on her front porch again. Before they died, she would sit there in the evenings and bring her radio outside so we could hear the fights. I think she really brought it out so that Ma Barnes, who lived next door, could hear the Joe Louis fights. They were friends.

But I decided that no, Mama only prayed to the Mother of Perpetual Help when she needed help with the family, like when Jackie jumped down from the low roof of McCreery's shed and caught his hand on a spike fence and had a big hole in his palm. I hoped she was praying for Daddy to come home. We hadn't seen him for what seemed like a long time.

After a while I didn't hear the Latin or the rosaries any more; I was dancing in a movie, wearing a red gown with gold flickering through it. By the time I woke up and we came out of church the magic of the soft day was gone and it was just a regular day.

Mary and I were sitting on the front steps watching the Protestants coming home from church. They came home much later than we did and we liked to see how they were dressed. Most of the time they wore clothes that were sort of ordinary but sometimes we could see the creases in them like they had been in a drawer all week. Today we were startled to see Mrs. Krantz wearing a yellow straw hat and an ugly house dress.

"I wonder if she's on welfare now?" I said. "she always had a nice blue dress before." "And that hat!" Mary said. "I don't think Mama would ever wear it even to six o'clock mass."

Nobody notices what you wear to that mass at six in the morning. You could have holes in your gloves or your hat could be frayed around the edges and it didn't matter; there were always other people dressed worse than you. Mary didn't usually go to early mass because she always kept her clothes nice, unlike me. Mama called me Sloppy Weather Annie. Maybe the Protestants who didn't have many clothes just didn't go to church.

"Let's go look at the Holy Rollers church," Mary said. Neither of us knew why everybody called it Holy Rollers, we never saw anybody rolling around. It was a little brick building that stood all by itself, not pushing up against each other like our house was on both sides. It was near the Brighton show so we looked at the posters showing Gene Autry along the way. I didn't like to admit that I liked him. Mary thought cowboy movies were dumb. Well, I guess they were but I liked the singing ones, like the ones Gene Autry made.

The windows of the church were open, the window sills were low enough that we could lean on them and see the whole room. Old wooden pews were laid out at angles to each other but there were no kneelers, and the rest of the room was bare, without even an altar. A Man in a white cassock stood before a music stand, waving his hands back and forth like a band director.

The people were standing in front of the pews, swaying and singing; the long, colorful dresses that men and women wore were swinging to the rhythm of the music. They had their eyes closed and they were all smiling and laughing. The colors of the people's clothes moved and sparkled in the sunlight that filled the room. I wanted to go in and shout out some songs too.

"No," Mary said. "We would go to hell if we went to any kind of church but a Catholic one." I wondered if God wouldn't like this better than the quiet and dark inside of the Catholic church. I guess he would if he was like me.

Some of the things about going to our church were nice, like the crib at Christmas time and listening to the music and singing the hymns and looking at the statues and the stained glass windows. Other things, like the sermons that went on and on forever and most of all, confession, I could do without. On Fridays, everybody in school was marched over to church where we filed into pews next to the confessional and waited for our turn to confess our sins. I usually worried that I didn't have enough sins to confess and had to make up some like I disobeyed my mother or I hit my brother, which I did but they didn't seem like sins to me.

The first Friday after school started I didn't have to make up any sins. The evening before I had been sitting on the front steps when Cherie came over. She danced across the bricks, carefully smoothed the skirt of her dress, touched the ribbon in her blond curls, and sat down on the cement step. Even though she lived right next door this was so unusual that I was speechless. I touched my hair, wished I had a ribbon in it, pulled my faded dress over my knees and waited to hear what she wanted.

"My Dad is home," she said after she was all settled. "He was on a job out west." I had never seen her father in the back porch and visualized him riding a horse through the plains, his hair falling over his forehead, cowboy hat shading his face, holding the reins loosely, like Gene Autry singing some haunting cowboy song like "I'm A Lone Cowboy."

Cherie swung her knees back and forth under the skirt of her yellow organdy dress. I didn't say anything. "I saw your father coming home last night," she said.

I pictured Daddy coming up the sidewalk, staggering a little, singing a lonely Irish song to himself. How could she have seen him? Was she looking out of her window? She stopped moving her knees and looked at my face, as if she couldn't wait to hear what I had to say.

"Well, I guess he was out on a job," I mumbled.

"Oh?" There was a question in her voice. "What kind of work does he do?"

"Oh." I wished I could say "pogamahoon" or some other Irish swear word. She wouldn't know what it meant and neither did I but I knew it was a bad word. How could I tell her the truth, which was that Daddy had not been on a job, but probably drinking down on the North Side. "Well, it was a job plumbing," I said. "He's a plumber, you know." Sometimes he was a plumber's helper, the one who dug the ditches for the plumbers to lay the pipe. I wasn't about to tell her that, either.

Mama must have heard my voice, because she called me

into the house. "What were you telling her?" she asked, and without waiting for an answer she said: "You talk too much!"

"But Mama," I said, "we were only talking about school."

"School!" She stood, hands on hips, a wet dish rag in one hand and a big spoon in the other, looking at me sidewise out of half closed eyes, as if she didn't believe me. "Don't you have enough of that at school? Haven't I told you often enough not to talk to the neighbors about us?"

I felt like crying but I was learning to be stubborn too. I looked back at her with my version of 'The Look' arms folded across my breast, chin tilted toward the ceiling, staring at her. My version lasted about two seconds and then I started crying. "I really wasn't talking about us, Mama," I wailed. "We really were talking about school! And now she'll never come and sit on our step again!"

"Thank the good Lord for that favor," she said, moving back to the stove. "We'll say no more about it."

I was amazed that she believed me. The lie was the worst I had ever told and for a moment I felt the flames of Hell rising up around me. I never thought I would lie to Mama. And this was a real lie, not a fib. Fibs were unimportant, small ones that didn't matter, like telling Cherie about Daddy. Part of it could have been true. He was a plumber's helper and sometimes he did work. Now I hated Cherie for making me tell my first real lie because I wanted to talk to her and have her for a friend. That's what I knew I had to lie to Mama about, and I hated Cherie for making me do it.

At confession time, I tried to sit near the confession box in case somebody would talk loud enough for me to hear them. This time I stayed to the back of the line so I would be the last one to confess, or be able to sneak out without confessing at all. This, of course, was impossible. Our Sister, the one who taught our class, stood at the end of each pew until everybody in the row stood in single file beside the confessional. I was doomed.

When my turn came, I turned the door knob, hesitantly went into the dark box, knelt down on the little kneeler, folded my hands and whispered, "Bless me Father, for I have sinned."

"Come, come," said the priest, "speak up. Don't be afraid." Well, I was afraid, but the Sisters said the priest was a representative of God so I thought I had to obey him. The other kids were right outside in the pews, trying to hear every word, so I raised my voice only slightly and started the ritual list of sins that I repeated every week.

"I hit my sister."

"I talked back to my mother."

"I talked in school."

Three things were sometimes enough to keep him from asking: "Is that all, my child?" If that happened I would have to make up another little sin or say: "Yes, Father," which might be a mortal sin because I couldn't tell him about the lie that I told my mother. I didn't know much about venial sins but even less about mortal sins. If I told a lie that might be a venial would two lies be a mortal sin? If I kept adding more lies was there something worse that a mortal sin?

"Is that all, my child?" the priest asked.

"Yes, Father," I mumbled.

"Your sins are forgiven you. May God bless you." The voice came closer as he spoke. I could see light from the open carvings in the confessional door reflecting on his raised hand. The blessing seemed like just another lie that was laid upon me. I knelt there, frozen to the hard wooden kneeler, waiting for the blast that would condemn me to hell. The only hope I had was that God might understand. If he knew everything, like the Sisters said he did, he knew why lies multiplied.

"You may go," the priest said. I crept out the door, keeping my head down to avoid looking at all my classmates who, I was sure, were watching me shuffle to my seat and snickering at me, the sinner.

Every night our family said the rosary. We each knelt down in front of a kitchen chair and were supposed to kneel up straight and not bend down over the seat. Even Daddy occasionally joined in this ritual. Mama started the praying, saying the first part of each prayer and we answered with the second. It started with The Apostle's Creed, a long one that didn't have an answer. Then the Our Father, three Hail Marys, a Glory Be to the Father and then the real chore - the mysteries. There were fifteen mysteries in all; The Glorious, The Sorrowful and The Joyous. We did one set of five mysteries a night, separated by a repetition in five sets of ten of the other prayers. The monotonous tone seemed to go on forever as Mary's clear, quiet voice lead the rest of us in our various mumbling answers. Anybody that slouched got a poke in the back from Mama. Except Daddy, of course. And maybe Jackie.

And we could never be sure what Mama would add on after that; sometimes a few more Hail Marys and sometimes we just had to kneel there while she finished her whispering prayers.

So lying to Mama was not a good idea. I was beginning to think that I could never be as good as her. She accepted her faith as part of her life. She thought of her religion as she thought of food: it was necessary and some of it you liked and some it you didn't, but you had to eat to keep alive, like it or not. I never thought of what those prayers meant to her, though. They were probably a desperate plea for help, and a firm belief that the Blessed Mother would provide it. The rosary was the food that she learned to savor in the desolate land of western Ireland, and the Church and the rosary were the connections to that world.

Post Traumatic Stress Disorder

Post traumatic stress disorder (PTSD) is among only a few mental disorders that are triggered by a disturbing outside event.

Many people experience individual traumatic events ranging from car and airplane accidents to sexual assault and domestic violence, which cause a cascade of psychological and biological changes. Simply put, it is a state in which you 'can't stop remembering.'

Although the disorder must be diagnosed by a mental health professional, symptoms of PTSD are clearly defined. You must have been in a situation in which you were afraid for your safety or your life, or you must have experienced something that made you feel inescapable fear, helplessness or horror.

Recent research has shown that PTSD changes the biology of the brain. Magnetic Resonance Imaging (MRI) and Positron Emission Tomography (PET) scans show changes in the way traumatic memories are stored in the brain.

CHAPTER TWELVE

Ask Me No Questions, I'll tell You No Lies

When Delia's first baby was born Mama told them that one of us could help Delia with the housework for a while. By this time I was considered old enough to go places by myself. Mary was responsible for Margie and Joe when Mama wasn't home so I was elected. "Make sure they give you some money," Mama said.

Ian and Delia lived with his aunt in her house, a large yellow brick one in that section of East Liberty where the houses were spread out with lots of space between them. There was a side path that led to a big back yard, and a back porch. The front of the house was far above the street level and you had to climb about twenty steps to get to the front door. The front porch shaded the house and the rooms in front were made even darker with heavy curtains. The kitchen was bright with filmy curtains on the two big windows; it was the only room in the house that wasn't dreary.

Mama and I had visited once before the baby was born and Mama would never go back again. The Aunt, for that was the only name Mama called her, was fat and wore a black dress with long folds flowing to the floor when she sat in the big arm chair. We spent most of the time sitting on hard chairs in the living room listening to her tell about the terrible things President Roosevelt was doing to our country. "Just look at what he's doing," she said, "using our hard earned money to give to people who are too lazy to help themselves!"

I was surprised that Mama didn't say a word when the Aunt said that. Franklin D. Roosevelt was revered almost as much as God in our house. When he became president he started programs to help those who had lost their jobs, their houses, and a way to find food for their families. Up to that time the government gave no help to people who were "down and out", in Mama's words. "That WPA is a plot to steal from people like us!" was the aunt's next comment. I could only look at her and wonder how she could say such things. The only work Daddy had done for a long time was with the Works Progress Administration and WPA was like a magic symbol to me. I didn't know what the letters meant but Daddy brought money home sometimes and I associated it with the welfare which kept us in food and clothes, even if the clothes were ones I wouldn't buy if I had money.

Mama had her say on the way home. "Sure they can say those things about President Roosevelt" she said while we were waiting for the street car. "They have lots of money and they keep it for themselves. That old Aunt, sitting there like the Queen of England, telling poor people that Roosevelt is no good! Thank God and the blessed Mother I don't have to visit her again!"

But I did. Delia asked Mama to have me baby sit for her one Sunday.

I used Daddy's Sunday pass and took the streetcar to Delia's house. The old aunt answered the doorbell. "Delia," she called when she saw me, "here's one of them young ones from over there on the Northside !" She motioned me in, muttering something in Irish, pushed the door closed, went into the room on one side of the hall and banged that door shut, too.

Delia looked thin. She was wearing a dark blue dress that was bunched around the waist with a belt and a straw hat that she wore straight on her head, not tilted like Mama's usually was. "The old lady is coming to church with me," she said. "Himself, (meaning Ian), is at work. The baby is sleeping so you can just listen for her, she'll sleep till we get back. So don't worry."

I had cared for Joe ever since he was a baby so I wasn't worried about what to do if she did wake up. Delia hurried down the hall, knocked on the living room door, waited while the aunt heaved her bulk up from the chair and held the old lady's cane as she guided her out the door and down the steps. I closed the heavy door after they reached the sidewalk, shattering the bit of light that came through the beveled glass at top, forming little streaks of dancing rainbows.

I wandered out to the kitchen, stood by the window and looked out at the yard. It had grass and a path going out to the end of the yard; a tree was close to the back fence, not a weak looking one with thin leaves like grew in our next door neighbor's yard but one with a big round trunk and leaves that were broad and offered the prospect of lots of shade.

I checked the dining room, a big room with a huge table covered by lace tablecloth and chairs arranged precisely along the sides. There were no pictures on the walls, not even one of the Sacred Heart or the Blessed Mother. I peeped into the living room; it was as dark as the hall. I was afraid to go in.

I finally decided to go upstairs and check the baby. She was in a crib in the bedroom on the second floor and was sound asleep, lying on her stomach. Wishing I had brought a book I looked around the room but there was nothing to read. I started down the steps to go back to the kitchen, thinking there might be something to read there. I was halfway down when I heard the lock turn in the front door. I was so startled that I couldn't think for a minute;, then ran into the baby's room, closed the door and leaned against it, wondering if it was a burglar.

"Delia?" It was Ian. I was so relieved that I threw open the door and called out: "It's me!" He was standing at the bottom of the steps, his coat over his shoulder, looking up toward me. As I started down he said: "Well, now. I had to leave work early and here you are to greet me." He stood there for a minute. "Stay there," he said: "I have something to show you."

I waited while he went into his room and dropped his coat on the bed. I was curious. Even though Mama didn't like him I always thought he was sort of glamorous, and he was the only person except my father who told me I was pretty. "Come on," he said, and started up the narrow stairs to the attic. When I didn't move he came back and took my hand. "Aren't you the pretty girl?" he said, holding my hand so tightly I couldn't pull away.

The attic room had one small window, the light casting shadows on the boxes and trunks scattered about. We crossed over the bare floor to a small trunk with brands bands across the rounded top. He kept my hand in his and with his other hand lifted the lid and took out a worn, tattered book as big as one of the tablets we used at school and started flipping through it. He now had his arm firmly around my waist, holding tighter as I tried to twist away from the unfamiliar pictures of men and women with no clothes on. He pointed to one picture. "See the number they make?" he asked. I wouldn't look at it; he turned my head so I would have to see it. "See," he said, "it makes the number 69. Did ever see a picture like that?" Before I could turn my head away again I saw the bodies of a man and a woman lying heads to feet with their heads slightly bent and 69 became a number that I could never look at again without thinking of those figures that looked like a huge, twisted frog.

He put the book down and held my face in his hand, turning it toward him. "You are a pretty little thing," he said and began kissing me, forcing his tongue between my teeth, his lips sloppy and wet. I tried to pull away again but he held me tighter and started fumbling with his pants. With the pants loosed, his suspenders hitting against my leg, he pushed against me.

"Look at me!" he commanded. I looked at his face and he pressed harder with his body, his eyes half closed, his lips clenched as he pushed and pushed, pulling my dress up and my pants down so I could feel something hard and damp between my legs.

A noise from downstairs made him pause and move away from me. "Christ! the front door! What's she doing home?" He pushed me away and hurriedly buttoned his pants, threw the book back into the trunk and closed it quietly. "Get downstairs before she gets the door open!" I could not move and kept staring at him. "Do as you're told!" he said in a low growl. He gave me a shove and I stumbled down the attic steps, my underpants hampering my movements. I stopped at the bottom, unable to go any further. He pushed me aside as he hurried down the other steps, pulled up his suspenders and grabbed his jacket from the bed in his room.

I heard the front door close and Delia came into the hall. "And what are you doing home?" she asked Ian as she passed the stairway on the way to the kitchen. "And where's Anna? Did she leave?"

"She's taking a last look at the baby," his answer sounded far away.

I raced down the stairs and out the door, leaving it open behind me. I wanted to cry but couldn't; I still had to go home on the streetcar. By the time I got to the stop I was able to think about the streetcar pass and found it in my pocket, bent and wrinkled.

My mother's first words when I got home were: "What are you doing home?" I stared at her. What did she mean? That's what Delia said to Ian. I live here, I thought. Where else would I go?

"What are you staring at me for?" Mama asked. Was she mad at me, too? How did she know? Did she know about the pictures? And the other?

"You didn't stay very long," she said when I didn't answer. "Did you get some money?"

I had forgotten about the money. "No."

"Well, then," she said, "you'll just have to go back and get it, Miss."

"No!"

"You'll get no! And a good thumping with it! That money will get us bread and milk!"

"I lost it." I said, my heart beating wildly. Another lie on top of everything else! I don't care, I thought. I'm not supposed to tell what happens in the family. How can I tell her about this? Or tell anybody else?

"Lost it? I've a good mind to thump you anyhow!" I just looked at her. I couldn't even cry. Then she gave a big sigh and looked at me, the lines of her face softening. Maybe I could tell her, maybe she would understand. But the thought passed.

"Ah, well. No use crying over spilt milk." she said.

The American Legion Medal

The American Legion School Medal Award is the highest honor awarded American youth by the American Legion. It is a medal that proclaims to the world that this boy or girl is the kind of young person we believe worthy of such an honor. The purpose of the program by the American Legion is the cultivation of high character and wholesome ideals in youth approaching active citizenship.

CHAPTER THIRTEEN

Revival

The trauma affected my emotional life, already damaged by the need for secrecy in our family and my penchant for hiding from unsettling situations. I had a mind, but it was closed to anything involving emotions. Because I was smart, others assumed that I knew what I was doing. I could see them, but not myself. I took care of what I could see and what my mother and the church told me I should see. I knew only "should", what I thought I should do. How this trauma affected my life was largely unknown to me. I had no self-knowledge, no feedback from others to help me understand my own wants and needs.

I remember sometime in the eighth grade, sitting at a desk in a classroom of a small, white wooden building across from our school. It may have been the original Annunciation parish school house that was occasionally used for classes. The top of the desk was crisscrossed with scratches and I was trying to figure out what some of the scratches meant. Sister Somebody had her back to us and was writing something on the board.

"Hey," the boy across from me said in a loud whisper. He leered at me, half leaning out of his chair. "You got golf balls!" he said.

I looked at his face, his grin, his eyes focused on my chest. He snickered and pointed at Dorothy, who sat in front of me and was primly watching the Sister at the board. Dorothy was one of those girls that was sweet and pretty and blinked her eyes at any boy within range, and I envied her. I knew little about how other girls felt. I had not been able to allow myself to be friend enough to talk much with any of the ones in my class.

William, that was his name, made gestures pointing at his own chest and moving his hands round and round. "She has tennis balls," he said. I was flooded with embarrassment when

I realized that the gestures meant her breasts were bigger than mine. His gestures reminded me of the picture that Ian showed me at his house. My face felt hot and flushed. William started to laugh and I put my head down on my arms on the desk. I wanted to rush out of the room and find a place to hide.

"William, what's so funny?" Sister asked, holding the eraser in her one hand and the chalk in the other. I hoped she might throw the eraser at him, as she sometimes did, but I was afraid to look and see. She didn't, and the next thing I heard was Sister's voice.

"Anna, wake up and pay attention!" she yelled. I raised my head and she glared at me as if it was my fault.

Eighth grade was almost over when another crucial event marked the end of that miserable year. I was to receive the American Legion medal. I could not understand why I was getting it and did not consider asking anybody for fear they would think I was dumb not to know already. When I brought it home and read what it meant I still did not understand why I received it. Scholarship, if that meant being smart in school subjects, I accepted. But the other reasons-- honor, service, Americanism, leadership and courage could not have been easily applied to me. I wasn't too sure I had any of those qualities; in fact, I was pretty sure I didn't. Maybe it was because my sister Mary got the medal when she graduated from eighth grade that they gave me one.

But they awarded it to me and I still have the medal. It has my name engraved on it, so I was proud but could not admit it out loud. The man who handed it to me made a speech but I didn't hear a word of it. Standing on the top step above the school yard I recited the thank you speech that the principal wrote for me with every kid in the school there watching. I'm sure William was there thinking about my golf balls and not about how smart and honorable I was.

We were a little more prosperous after I graduated from the eighth grade. Mama was working as a cook at Oliver High School, a few blocks away on Brighton Road.

"It's easier than scrubbing floors at Montefiore Hospital," she said, "but it doesn't pay much." But at least she didn't have to walk three miles each way when she didn't have street car fare. It seemed like she had scrubbed floors for as long as I could remember. I hated that she had that job. I didn't know anybody else whose mother scrubbed floors.

Mama was home all that summer and we had to help her with house cleaning. Even Margie and Joe were included in some of the jobs. I remember them quietly sitting on the floor the day we took up the living room carpet. It was a lovely blue one just the color of the cloak on the statue of the Blessed Mother. We carefully rolled up the carpet and Jackie and Mama carried it into the back yard where Mama beat it viciously with a carpet beater, an instrument made of stiff wire about the size of a plate with a wooden handle to grasp it. All of us, including Margie and Joe, helped to pick up the last year's newspaper used for padding under the rug.

We sorted out the brittle sheets, but Betty was kneeling, throwing paper in every direction. Finally Mary got mad and said: "Stop it! You're getting everything wrinkled!"

"I want the comics," Betty said.

"Sit down and when we find them we'll read them to you." Mary took her by the hand and dragged her over to sit on the bare floor.

We finally sorted out the comics and the movie pages and tossed the ones with the news onto the pile that was to be put in the rubbish. Comics were always good. We, with the possible exception of Mary, were not interested in hearing about Hitler and the lingering depression, and 1939 seemed like ancient history. So we read the old comics like "Joe Palooka" out loud yelling "youse" and "ain't" at the top of our lungs, words called slang by Mama and usually forbidden in our house.

"Read it again!" Betty would yell. Jackie was back from helping Mama with the rug by this time and he joined the chorus. We read "Apple Mary", about a woman who sold apples on the streets of New York, a comic that was almost as impressive as "Joe Palooka."

"Let's read Mama's story!" Betty called out. She was holding up one of the comic pages which had the daily story about love and romance that Mama set aside to read when she was in bed.

"Mama doesn't allow us to read that," Mary said. I didn't mind. I always read her stories anyhow and couldn't see what she liked about them.

But Mama came back, looking for Jackie to help carry the carpet back in to the house. So we gathered up the old papers, Mary swept the floor and we put new pages down in the same place, making sure to put the comic pages on top for the next time we cleaned the carpet.

I started keeping a diary in early 1942. World War Two had started in December, 1941 and someone suggested that writing a war journal would be a good idea, although I wrote little about the war after the first few pages. I did not consciously realize that the diary was filling the need to communicate with somebody, and that somebody had to be myself since I could not develop other avenues. I was beginning to see some classmates as friendly rather than disinterested, but found it impossible to reach out to them. I started to write the things I might have told a friend if I had one. It was only after I read the diaries years later that I was able to understand more deeply how the circumstances of my life affected me during that time.

I didn't write about Daddy in the journal. The more I thought about him the less I wanted to think about him. He was not real any more. He didn't sing under his breath while reading the encyclopedia. He didn't come in and say "Hello, Mecushla" like he used to. He didn't eat with us when he was home. I didn't want to admit that he was a drunkard. When I asked Mama why he was like this, she never had any answer but a shrug. He worked occasionally with the WPA, doing labor in county parks and sometimes brought money home. Even when he gave Mama some of the money, she yelled at him for not having more. When he was gone for weeks at a time life was calmer but even then I couldn't bring anybody to our house because I was afraid he would come in drunk.

"Can't you just not let him come home?" I asked once. Again, her shrug was the answer.

School had been out for what seemed like ages. The morning was still cool and I walked up the street to where it turned a corner so sharp that it looked like the street ended. I walked to school that way but never paid attention to what it looked liked after the end of our block. Rose, a girl from my class who lived in the next block, was coming out of her house with some friends. She saw me and said they were going for a walk up to Perry Highway, a mile on the other side of our school, and asked me if I wanted to go along. I was sure that she was asking me because the other girls were there but I said yes. We walked for a long time and came to a place along the road where flowers bloomed in great bunches on the side of the road and far into the fields beside it. There must have been hundreds of orange ones flaunting themselves on the curb, leaning over to the street and waving in the air stream of passing cars.

"What are they?" I asked Rose.

"They're tiger lilies. Haven't you ever seen tiger lilies?" one of her friends answered. They kept on walking but I stood there, entranced by the brilliance of the color, the seemingly unending mass of them; the slight movements as if they were dancing. I thought I had never seen such a beautiful sight and was deeply excited by the unexpected impact of the exotic, brilliant color stretching on and on. Long after the others were gone I was still watching. They may have said goodbye but I wasn't listening.

I had the same feeling on a day in the spring when I encountered the overwhelming fragrance of lilacs. A huge lilac displayed its blossoms over a black iron fence that I passed when I was going a different way home from school. The excitement was the same, it engulfed my whole being. The aroma was wonderful; it assaulted my mind. I could not ignore it; it smelled like heaven might smell. I could not leave that bush without taking a few of the blossoms with me. I didn't even think about what Mama would say if she knew so I had to drop them before I got home in case she thought I stole them.

I was undergoing a gradual awakening in a new world of the senses. I knew I loved the smell of warm bread that was home and warmth, and I knew the smell of the river, a rancid mixture of riverboat fuel and other substances that floated up when were crossing the bridge to downtown. I had never before encountered those senses in their full bodied extremes, in the heady fragrance and in the visual extravaganza of moving color. I think this awakening continued through my sophomore year. The joy that I felt about the flowers somehow was the beginning of a suspension of a belief that nobody would like me.

During those high school years I stayed home from school a lot and nobody seemed to notice. When I was in elementary school I was sick frequently, something that gave me a lingering cough, and missed a lot of school. I think Mama worried about tuberculosis, the illness that her brother had died from, so she never forced me to go. I stayed home to finish reading Gone With the Wind, to help Mama with housecleaning, to get our latest rationing stamps, or simply because I wanted to stay home for some unknown reason. It may have seemed like freedom, but now I realize that I felt that nobody, except my mother, paid attention to whether I was around or not. One time I skipped school and did some shopping on the North Side. On my way home, I got on the street car and found that my class had gone to a concert that day. "Oh, Anna's here," somebody said, as if I had been there all along.

At the same time I began to vaguely to wonder about my obligations toward church and religion. I went to Mass. There was no way to get around Mama's demands about that; she was still the most important figure in my life and even when I wanted to disobey her I had too much guilt to actually do it. The church still felt comfortable and familiar. The light filtering through the stained glass windows, the moving shadows from the flickering candles, the darts of flame reflecting in the golden halo of the filigreed monstrance, the blind eyes of the statues, the glittering vestments of the priest still commanded my attention but did not seem to have any relation to the God I feared. Confession was still confusing. I tried going a few times after the grade school monitoring ended in eighth grade but I felt like I was just telling more lies. I didn't think I was committing sins in my life and made them up when I did go.

Lent was still a season to be reckoned with. Mama said that we were to go to mass on Wednesdays. It didn't matter that we had to get up at six thirty to get to the church by seven thirty. I complained, but of course I went and Betty went with me. We stopped complaining when we found out that we were to get a nickel each morning to get some breakfast.

Each week for the six weeks of Lent we went to Petty's Bakery , a little building across from the church that had a white wood front and inside, rows of fresh baked goods lined up behind slanted glass showcases inside. We raced to get there before church and buy breakfast, a cruller for each of us. These were made of a dough like doughnuts are now made of, but they were three or four inches long and an inch or more thick, filled with a sweet cream filling and slathered with creamy chocolate on top. They were a little crisp on the outside and soft and luscious inside. The word ethereal comes to mind. I wonder if they were really that good? Maybe not, but it was another sensation that I was learning to treasure, the sensations that are the parts of that stage of my life that I remember most vividly.

By the time I reached my sophomore year in high school I was responding to friendly approaches from some of my classmates. Our class had the usual high school cliques and I watched and envied the ones who were in the favored clique. I tried to figure out what made them so favored. Katherine could fall backward and hit the floor without getting hurt; Betty always laughed a lot and was a good basketball player; Bette would wiggle her long fingers and bend them to the back of her hand.

Margeurite was the one I envied the most. She had long,

blond hair with a high pompadour rolled in front, cascading down the back on a wild mass of curls. She wore sweaters, usually pink, that clung tightly to her curves. She giggled when there was a boy around, and there were always boys around, except in school, of course. Annunciation High was for girls only so there was no opportunity there, but she took care of that by transferring to the public high school in her senior year.

I had straight brown hair that refused to stay in place. When I wore a sweater it fell straight to my hips. I wore it strictly for warmth. I was tall and skinny and unfortunately liked to read, giving me the reputation of being smart. But I thought Margeurite was smart. The one thing that the girls in that clique had in common seemed to be that they were friendly to each other and seemed oblivious of the rest of the us.

There was another group of girls who must have felt like I did, and they wanted to be part of a group like that. Dolores was one of those girls. Sometimes I walked home from school the back way, which passed Dolores's house. One day she walked with me and asked me if I would like to join her group. Her invitation gave me the same kind of excited feeling that I got when I saw those beautiful flowers. I think Dolores did more for me than I realized and I doubt if Dolores ever knew the effect that she had on me.

It was more than just friendship. Her mother had Parkinson's disease. She was in a wheel chair, her face was rigid, her arms and hands shook, sometimes violently, spittle came from her mouth when she tried to talk. Dolores treated her as if she was just like anybody else. She was not ashamed of her like I was of my father's drinking. Dolores talked to her mother about her day at school, she wiped her mother's face when it needed it, she invited friends to the house and we sat on her porch and talked to her mother, too. I felt ashamed of myself. And after knowing her for some time I told Mama that I wanted to invite the girls to our house for dinner.

"And isn't it about time you should ask somebody here?" was her response.

"What if Daddy comes home when they're here?" I asked. Or probably I didn't ask her that, I just worried that he might come home drunk and I didn't think I could be as nice about it as Dolores was to her mother.

So Mama made a big meal of spaghetti and meatballs. We never had spaghetti with anything but butter and I could not remember ever having meatballs. I don't like to think about how I felt embarrassed about the abundance of food that she served. But the girls were wonderful; they treated her just like they treated Dolores' mother. I hope I thanked Mama for it but I don't remember that I did.

I did not understand it at the time, but what I learned from Dolores was the beginnings of the value of thinking of somebody else and not always of myself. I was learning to respond to others and to admit to some positive things about myself.

That fall I wanted badly to get a job and was not having any success. The fact that I was not quite sixteen didn't help any. I decided to try a novena—nine days of going to church and praying to St. Theresa (Theresa is my middle name and I wasn't too sure that there was a St. Anna) to please get me a job. I contributed my last twenty eight cents to the Sunday church collection. I also lied on my application to Woolworth's 5 & 10 cent store, saying I was sixteen, which meant I would not have to get a working permit. Getting a working permit meant a long trip to the board of Education in Oakland, in the eastern part of Pittsburgh, with your birth certificate. Somehow that lie didn't seem to matter. What mattered more was to get a job like many of the other girls in my class were able to do. In spite of all my doubts, I got the job.

The assistant manager, Betty, was called the Floor Lady and was in charge of the first floor, where I was assigned. She had dyed blond hair, piled up on her head in a huge pompadour even higher than Margeurite's. She wore tight skirts and very tight sweaters, high heels and walked around swinging her keys. I was at a counter near the front of the store and customers would often pick up articles like reading glasses and put them down in the wrong place on the counter, leaving an empty space in the rows of glasses. Betty nagged at me to clean up my counter and told me that I was to put small blocks under the sections that looked empty so it would not look so bare. It seemed sort of dishonest and I wished that I had gotten a job at Kresge's, the 5 & 10 store next door, which was more prosperous. But I thought you probably had to have a working certificate before they would hire you there.

After awhile at Woolworth's I was switched to a busier counter, and became somewhat friendly with Kathy, the other girl there. We laughed at Betty's expense, especially at her way of telling us it was time to close up. "Put your buckets out, girls!" she would say every evening. This was a reference to the "fire buckets", filled with sand which was to be spread on a fire if one occurred. The buckets were kept under the counter during business hours and set out in the aisle so they would be easy to find in case of fire after hours. Some of the girls would turn their rear ends out toward the aisle and wiggle them when Betty called closing time, but she never seemed to notice the giggles or the extended rears.

I think Betty fascinated me because there was a constant rumor that she and Murph, the store manager, were having an affair. I began to like her. She was fair and almost always pleasant, and when she found out that I was only fifteen she didn't have me fired, just told me to get a working permit.

I worked there through the winter, making thirty three cents an hour, not an unusually low rate at the time. The job helped me. I was able to respond to some offers of friendship. I was beginning to feel some real sense of confidence in myself.

Remember Pearl Harbor

I don't remember Pearl Harbor
I remember our kitchen--
My mother standing in front of the stove
holding a large metal spoon
looking at the wall instead of the stew.
The smell of apple pie drifting from the oven.
Uncle Paddy sitting between the doors
to the dining room and hall,
 tilting the chair back against the wall.
Me thinking that's why they call it a chair rail.
Mama saying nothing about his perilous position.
Daddy and his brothers in a half circle around the stove
holding their caps, staring at the linoleum.
Betty and Margie leaning over the table, no longer arguing
over ownership of a Shirley Temple cutout,
turning to look at the radio announcing its solemn message.
Suddenly life seemed as precarious as the tilted chair,
as unknown as the silence and immobile figures.

Smaller War Plants and Cadet Nurses

Smaller War Plants Corporation was a U.S. agency established in June, 1942 as a division of the War Production Board. Its aim was to finance and aid smaller American businesses.

In 1943, the peak year of the U.S. production, firms with under a hundred employees were awarded 86,000 contracts.

Cadet Nurses of World War II were the largest and youngest group of uniformed women to serve their country during World War II and early postwar years from 1943-1948.

They served under the auspices of the United States Public Health Service. Qualified applicants were given scholarships that covered tuition, books, uniforms, partial room and board, and a small monthly stipend.

In return, Cadet Nurses pledged to actively serve in essential civilian, military or other Federal and governmental services for the duration of the war. They comprised 80% of the nursing staff for civilian hospitals during the war.

CHAPTER FOURTEEN

The Home Front

Sunday, December 7, 1941. All of us were in the kitchen, including Uncle Paddy, Mama's brother, and Uncle Eddie, Daddy's brother. Mama was cooking dinner and we were all very quiet, listening to the news, the radio high up on a shelf, safely away from the hands of children, and out of striking distance of missiles thrown in anger. President Roosevelt was telling us that the Japanese had bombed Pearl Harbor that morning and we were now at war.

I had the same feeling that I got when Mama and Daddy were fighting: a need to escape, to find a place where I could think about anything except what might happen. I thought with fear and apprehension of the pictures I had seen in newsreels of the bombing of Britain, of the stories and atrocities committed by the Nazis. Pittsburgh would surely be bombed; it was the center of the steel making industry. Everybody else must have been thinking the same thing but we just looked at the radio and said nothing.

The shock of Pearl Harbor changed the tempo of our lives. The war became the news that was reported every fifteen minutes on the radio. It was a tragedy for a large part of the world's population, but to some of us it was distant and barely intruded into our lives. It brought us out of the dreary depression of the thirties and gave us a chance to get jobs and make money. Our only sacrifice was rationing of food like sugar, coffee and tea. When the boys, as we called the servicemen, came home, the war gave us heroes to admire. For me, it dragged me out of the lethargy that had plagued me for the two years before.

As I began to wake up, I was still reading prodigiously and indiscriminately about other people's lives and how they lived. I was still scrubbing the kitchen every week, cleaning the bathroom as well, and going to the show with Mama as often as

I could talk her into it. Some of the movies were pretty awful but we went anyhow. They changed three times a week and always had a double feature, a movie labeled A and which had some well known star, and one released as a B movie, which had people that we had never heard of. At least once a week there was a form of bingo during an intermission between the movies. Mama would go even in Lent and if the movie was really bad she would say: "Well, that's what we get for going in Lent." I knew she liked a movie if she was quiet on the way home. If somebody like Joan Crawford or Barbara Stanwyck was in it she lingered for a while looking at the posters with their pictures on them.

Few people complained about the war. Rationing became a fact of life, the servicemen had to have the first and best of everything and people generally agreed with that and didn't complain. If anyone did complain the response more often than not was: "Don't you know there's a war on?" The war was always there, but life for those of us at home became better. Meat, eggs, milk, butter and other foods were rationed. I missed tea and sugar, both of which were not rationed but just hard to get. Mama got food no matter what during the depression and she got tea no matter what during the war. A lady on the lower North Side always had it available and periodically one of us would go to the tea lady and get a bag of tea. I don't know what Mama paid for it, we just picked it up.

It wasn't that we didn't pay attention to the war, but it became so much a part of our lives that we thought about it all the time. It was like talking about school or eating every day. It was background, like the blue sky and clouds that are on the screen saver on my computer now. It was as if that background was violence and bombing and planes and smokestacks spewing out dirty smoke and your nose always full of dirt and your clothes covered with soot by ten in the morning. And we were happy to have that black soot. The city was relatively clean during the depression but that meant that people were not working, and having a hard time getting food and clothing. By the second year of the war almost everybody was working at some job or was in the service or leaving school a semester early so they could join up as soon as they were eighteen.

Even the blackouts gave some moments of beauty. I remember looking out the front room window one time as the "all clear" sounded. The moon was brilliant; the single light from the street car coming around the bend and the lights blinking on a few at a time made the street look enchanted.

After I graduated from high school in 1944 I got a temporary summer job at Gimbels in downtown Pittsburgh. I was excited about it until I had worked there for about a week on an addressograph machine, a horror which punched names and addresses on small pieces of metal about the size of a modern credit card-- a predecessor of it, no doubt. I spent eight hours a day lifting a heavy metal arm up, dragging it down on the metal to print the image, removing the card and doing it again, on and on. I was making about sixty cents an hour and would have taken half that to escape that job.

One evening when I was trudging home after getting off the street car, I met George, a boy who lived across the street from us. He was enough older than me that I never paid any attention to him and I was sure that he never noticed me, so I was surprised when he stopped to talk to me. I always thought he was kind of ordinary looking, not as tall as Jackie, with what we called "dishwater blond" hair.

"Hi!" he said.

"Hi!" I said. It would have been rude not to answer. Anyway, boys coming up and saying hi was not something that had ever happened to me before.

"Are you working somewhere?" he asked.

"At Gimbels," I said.

"Do you like it?"

Since I had just been mulling over in my mind about how much I hated it "No!" came out pretty strongly.

"That's what I thought," he said, "you don't look as happy as you used to."

That stopped me for a minute. How did he know that?

He must have understood what I was thinking when I just looked at him.

"Oh, I come home about the same time that you do and see you walking up the street sometimes. How much do you make an hour?"

I was still thinking about him watching me walk up the street and told him. "Sixty cents an hour."

"I bet you would like a chance to make big money, wouldn't you?" Well, who wouldn't? I thought.

"Yes, who wouldn't?" I said.

"Well, I work at a war plant out in the North Hills. We need more workers and I thought you might be interested."

This needed some serious consideration so I gave it a minute. Anything would be better than Gimbels. "Yes," I said. "I'm interested."

"Okay," he said, "I'll pick you up at 7:30 tomorrow morning. Umm, you should know that this is a war plant and everything is very confidential." It seemed that all of life was about the war, so confidential was normal. Everything was blamed on the war. Besides, our whole family life was confidential. George may not have known much about my family, but he surely saw my father staggering home occasionally and knew that we didn't talk about it. It never occurred to me at the time that George probably liked me. My only thought was that I would call Gimbels and tell them I was sick.

So the next morning George showed up in a car. I wondered how he got a car, even an old one like that one was. The war had been going on for almost three years and only privileged people drove any kind of a car. Gasoline was rationed, too, so how did he get that? And where did he park it? I had never seen it on the street. Naturally, I began to wonder if he was a gangster, a rather romantic thought. He couldn't be, though. He was a neighbor and I felt kind of sorry for him because he was 4F, which meant he was not in military service because he had something wrong with him.

During the World War II men between the ages of

eighteen and thirty five had to register for the draft. Not all of the young men who registered were accepted into the service. About thirty percent of the registrations were rejected for physical defects, and were given the 4-F classification. Most people thought that any American man of weapon-bearing age not in the uniform of the armed services was believed to be a slacker, and called them 4-Fers.

My brother Jackie was unable to get into any of the services because of a ruptured eardrum that happened when he was small, when there was no treatment for ear infections. When the Merchant Marines turned him down, the only option left, he wouldn't even speak to us for a long time. He was classified as 4-F, which I think to him meant failure. And people were cruel. Often they would stop young men on the street and ask them why they were not serving their country. Jackie was ashamed of it and tried to pretend that it didn't matter, but it did. He got a job at Sear's Garage and never talked about it again.

George and I drove out Route 8 to an ugly, square, dirty looking building that looked empty. "It's called the Catalyst Research Company," George said. "Don't ask me what it means 'cause I don't know and anyhow we're not supposed to tell anybody where we work."

He led me through a long corridor that went straight through from the front to the back of the building. On each side of this hallway were large cubicles with open doorways and people standing inside of them apparently doing nothing.

"Here's our new recruit!" George called out to the man sitting in another, larger cubicle at the end of the row.

"O. K. George," he answered. "Bring her in here." It was all too sudden for me to be scared or even worried.

After a short interview with the manager, a harried looking individual who peered out at me from behind long grey bangs, he told me to bring my school records and a letter from somebody who knew me well.

"Tomorrow!" he said. I didn't have the nerve to ask how much I would get paid or even what I was going to do.

"Don't worry," George said when we were back in the car and heading home, "you'll like it. All you do is check on what's cooking in those glass containers that are lined up in each of the cubicles."

"What's in them?" I asked.

"Who knows?' he answered. "Probably stuff that they use to make bombs. And you'll have to sign a pledge not to tell anybody where you're working or anything about it."

Bombs! Secrets! That was pretty scary. All those posters with Uncle Sam pointing his finger telling people not to talk would be pointed at me. Then I thought about the addressograph machine and decided not to think about that part of it.

I took the next day off from work, went up to the school and got my record plus a letter from one of the sisters recommending me as an honest person, a good worker and student. How does she know I'm honest, I thought. I did not think of myself as a completely honest person. I couldn't remember her name and had never had her in class but was not about to argue my good luck.

When I called in to take another day off I was told that I would be fired if I took a third one. More good luck! I would never have to go back to that line of unfortunate girls banging away on those awful machines.

The interview was thorough. The manager asked me all kinds of questions about my family and where I was working. I was as honest as I could be under the circumstances, saying that my parents were Irish immigrants but I thought they were citizens. I had no idea if that part was true because I was unsure about my father's status, but he didn't question me further.

I had to hang around with nothing to read until lunchtime when George was to take me home. As we were leaving the manager stopped us and asked me if I would like to start the next week. My salary would be about ninety cents an hour, a pretty neat sum. I was hired even though I told them that I was going to nurse's training in the fall. And as a Cadet

Nurse I would be part of the military, so maybe that was also in my favor. Many of the men were leaving for the armed services after a short time so it was not a problem.

Each cubicle in the war plant had an aisle through the middle with glass vats sitting on burners on one side. These had large pieces of nickel immersed in mercury, at least it looked like mercury but I was never told that. These cooked until the nickel was melted. My job was to watch them and notify another person, a man, who would then remove them.

Lined up on the other side of the aisle were seven or eight beautiful glass containers that looked like elegant swans. Each one was filled almost to the curve of the neck with the liquid silver and mercury. The combination had a flat, solid look that moved lethargically when the flask was lifted and put into place over a heating element. The contents were heated for twenty four hours and gradually turned into black powder which, again, was removed and the whole process was started over again.

The job was completely boring. All I had to do was sit on a stool and watch the vats and the swans in case anything did happen. Nobody seemed to know what that might be. Whatever it was it never happened.

"Could they blow up?" I asked George one day when he was removing vats of melted nickel and setting up another row on the burners. He put a finger to his lips in imitation of Uncle Sam in the huge posters on every cubicle wall warning us to keep our mouths shut. I glanced occasionally at both sides of the aisle and went back to reading my current book, usually one of the numerous travel books by Richard Halliburton. His books told about the romantic things he did like swimming the Hellespont because he admired Byron, who had done the same thing years before. He traveled to India and gave loving description of the Taj Mahal and told about the princess whose memorial it was. He also visited Russia and told some romantic tales that were sad and gruesome about the murder of the royal family of Romanov. I learned quite a bit of history that summer.

One lunchtime was memorable. One of the men who worked there invited me to go for a ride with him on his motorcycle. Again, as I did when George asked me if I wanted the job, I said yes without further thought. "Hop on!" he said.

I sat on the little seat behind him, tucked my skirt under my legs, tentatively put my arms around his waist while he revved up the motor. "Hold on tighter!" he bellowed, "and don't let go, whatever you do!" My O. K. was lost in the roar of the engine as we pulled on to the road and quickly turned into the entrance of North park.

My experience in moving vehicles up to this time had been almost entirely on street cars. I was completely exhilarated with the speed, the magical merging of the scenery into swirling masses of color, the warm feel of the man's skin under his light shirt, the sharp sensation of the wind against my own skin. I believe now that the fragrance of the lilacs, the vision of the orange flowers and the touch of the man's skin in the wind unveiled senses that I had blocked and allowed me to begin to admit to myself other feelings and emotions that I was unfamiliar with.

Even though Mama had always told me that I would be a nurse I made the decision myself to join the Cadet Nurse Corps. I would get three years of training for free, another wartime benefit. Mama was pleased. "You'll always have something to fall back on," she said. One of her employers before she got married offered to pay for her to study nursing and she turned it down. "To my sorrow," I had heard her say many times.

Daddy's response on my last day of work at the war plant was quite different. "Why in the name of God are ye leaving such a good paying job?" he asked. I had no answer for him. He had never given me advice before and I had no way to respond to him then.

My mother's last words to me on the day I left were "And don't come back!" At least that is what my not always reliable memory insists she said. I was only going to St. Joseph's

Hospital on the other side of the city, two street car rides away. I would be coming home on weekends for the first six months, have a month's vacation in the summer, and be home two days a week after that. Mama often let her feelings be known in her actions, and tossed out brusque statements that covered over what she really felt. I had always understood her actions better than her words. In my mind that "And don't come back" meant that I better not quit. For the next few years while I was in nursing school, she made apple pie for me every time I came home, which was a loving thing for her to do. But her words, whether they were imagined or spoken, lingered on and plagued me throughout my years of nurses training.

After the first six months of reading and studying, student nurses were assigned to what was called floor duty. Celi, another nurse in my class and I were assigned duty on the second, or men's floor. It was considered the most demanding unit in terms of skills needed to function well. I was pleased with the assignment and thought Celi and I were there because we had both done well in our preliminary studies. We were told to go back to the ward and introduce ourselves.

We walked down a dimly lit corridor to the ward, a large room for patients with similar problems. There were about twenty beds, ten or so on each side. One wall was filled with windows, flooding the whole room with light. Most of the men in the ward were in bed but a number of them were standing, using a cane for support, or sitting in a small group at the end of the aisle. There was a moment of silence when we entered, then a storm of whistles and shouts erupted. I stood frozen, not knowing what to say or do, but Celi just smiled.

The noise slowed and then stopped. We walked down the aisle Celi leading and stopping at every bed, introducing us saying things like "How are you?" when the patient looked like he could respond, and touching the hand of some who were asleep or unable to talk. I said little and felt uncomfortable until some of the men sitting on chairs told me how glad they were to see us.

"Don't mind these guys," one of them said. "They like to see pretty new faces." I blushed, but Celi just laughed.

The second floor was for men only. It was filled with patients who had severe illness, like heart or lung disease, fractures or loss of limbs from accidents on their jobs. Most of the men worked in the mills, some of them were older men called back to work when the younger men were drafted.

A large number of those men needed alcohol to enable them to function. Drinking was a normal part of their lives, they worked hard and drank hard. The unit had what was called the whiskey cupboard, a locked closet beside the chart room, where the liquor brought in by friends or relatives was kept. It was doled out once a day, in the evening, unless the recipient seemed to be developing delirium tremens, caused by withdrawal of alcohol following habitual excessive drinking. Nobody, staff or patient, wanted that to happen, so the alcohol was increased as needed. Occasionally some of the whiskey would disappear from the cupboard and the patient's family would complain that some staff member was more needy than the patient.

The men were often loud, raucous, and intimidating. I could not be like Celi and respond to their jokes and innuendoes with laughter, and was unable to function using the skills that I had studied so hard to learn. We had a teacher, Sister Amadeus, who taught and supervised us when we were working on the units, and she must have suggested to the floor supervisor that I was not ready for the demands of that floor and I was transferred. I never knew why and never asked.

This was a major setback for me. I thought I was able to control my life but I was failing and was afraid that I would have to leave. I had no alternatives and was panic stricken. Fortunately I was sent to the third floor where the women patients were generally kind, happy to be in the hospital getting care, and appreciative.

There was never a mark against my record. It was my own anxiety that made me think that I was a failure. But the anxiety did not go away. I worried every day that I really might fail.   I studied hard to learn every skill, practiced memorizing every part of a treatment,   made lists so I would not forget important things.

I discovered a secret: that I pretended a lot. I pretended that I was not worried; I pretended that I could do things that I was not sure I could do; I pretended that I was confident. The patients believed me, the staff believed me, the supervisor must have believed me because she left me alone a lot of the time and never questioned me.

Even though I could do the job, the problem with all of this pretending was that I could not disguise my emotions from myself. I felt them. Every day started with fear of what might happen. The consequence for me was that I formed a mindset that was based on fear of the future.   I have never been able to completely change that. Eventually I was able to abandon the pretending because I really did know the nursing and other necessary skills. But the fear remained all through my working days as a nurse and still shows up when I experience something new and traumatic. I lose control and then I panic. I am back in that room with Ian, Delia's boyo, and I don't know how to cope with what is happening to me.

The Spring House

When I found the spring
I sat on the damp stone
drank cool water from my cupped hands
scattered a few drops on the ground
remembering the ancient god that Merlin found,
and wishing for my Dad to find us.

CHAPTER FIFTEEN

The New House

"Of course we do!" Mary said. "We have to move."

We had been paying rent for the house on Charles Street for years. I never knew the amount, but it wasn't very much, I guess. We used to own the house, but when the depression got bad Mama didn't have enough to pay on the mortgage, and we lost it. The Building and Loan Association took it over, but they let us stay and rent it until it was sold. And now it was sold.

It was 1945, the war in the Pacific was not over yet but I guess people had more money and started buying those houses that the banks owned.

Mary pulled at a ringlet of hair, which meant that she was thinking. "I wonder ..." She stopped and I waited to hear what new idea she had. "I wonder if we could buy a house. Jackie and I have a little money. Mama lets me keep anything I have after I save enough for school and she lets Jackie keeps some of what he makes. I'll talk to him." Jackie had quit school at sixteen and was working in a garage while Mary was working in an office to pay for college.

"Mmmm." Mary was still thinking. "Maybe Mama has some money," she finally said. Mama was working at a restaurant on Forbes Street in downtown Pittsburgh. "Sometimes the food she brings home saves her some money. I guess they feel sorry for somebody with six kids and a drunken husband."

"Don't call him that," I said, knowing full well she was right. I just didn't like to hear it said out loud.

"Well, what would you say? When does he ever bring money home? Who's doing the worrying about a place to live? Not him, you can be sure. Mama only hollers at him because he spends it on his drunken friends. You know we'd be better off if he wasn't here."

"But Mary." I could say no more. My stomach was

heaving and I wanted to cry. I didn't want to hear what Mary was saying. Even though I heard it often I didn't want to believe it. When I was little I thought Daddy was kind and gentle. He told wonderful stories about Ireland and gangsters and copper mines in Montana. Had he changed so much? Or was it me? Would we really have to move to a strange place because of him? I was in a strange place myself and it seemed like the whole world was changing around me. I was home for the summer break from the hospital and had enough problems that I couldn't seem to solve.

"Will Daddy come?" I asked. There was no answer to that, either.

Later that evening I listened to Mary telling Mama about a house that she and Jackie had looked at. "There must be something about it," Mama was saying. "Why else would they be selling it for practically nothing?"

"It's only the down payment that's low," answered Mary. "Jackie said that this guy at work told him about it. It's been empty for a long time and they want to sell it." Mama looked at her with that sideways look that meant she didn't believe that.

"Well," Mary asked, "how long did it take the Building & Loan to sell this one?"

"Eight years," Mama said. "But that's different. They stole it from me. Who would buy a house when everybody knows how those people got it?" She made a growling noise in her throat. "I worked for years to get the money for this house," she said, "just to lose it to some millionaires who went around taking poor people's homes."

Mary sighed audibly. I knew why. We had heard the story often enough. Now we would hear about the good furniture Mama had to sell for almost nothing, the dishes that were wedding presents and were gone, too. The years that they were on welfare, the bills at the grocery store. She didn't say any more this time, though. She only asked about the payments.

"I don't know how different it is," Mary said. "But when we went to see him the owner asked us how much we could pay a month. If we can get a hundred together for the down payment, Jackie and I can help some with the monthly payments."

"Ora Musha, we don't have a hundred dollars!" Mama lapsed into Irish, the language that came into her mind when she was very upset or angry. "Even with the little bit we got from your father and counting what you and Jackie have it only comes to eighty one dollars." Her sigh was just like Mary's had been a few minutes before.

"Just come with us tomorrow, Mama. Please. We have to have you. He won't talk to us any more without you."

"I'll go," Mama said, "but this two dollar bill your father brought into the house won't bring us any luck." She laid the bill on the table and smoothed it out with her fingers, carefully straightening the corners, turning it over and over, as if that would change it into something lucky. We watched her in silence. Finally she slapped it with her palm, pushed back from the table and said: "God help us, we will go and see what they say. Betty can watch Margie and Joe." Mama looked at me. "I'm going," I said. She shrugged her shoulders.

We walked across North Side streets until we got to Federal Street., then walked up the long hill to another hill, up that and climbed another, even steeper than the first two. We passed a group of two story buildings scattered on one side of the street, the other side was covered with trees and bushes straggling down a steep incline to the road below. I felt like they had dropped the whole city into the valley we had just left. I had never seen so many trees outside of the cemetery, and they were real trees, not old sumac bushes like we had in the backyards on Charles Street.

"There it is!" Mary said as we rounded a bend in the road. A huge tree almost obscured a soft red brick house. It looked romantic, like Tara, Scarlet O'Hara's house in Gone With the Wind. There was a long porch across the front shading two large windows, one on each side of the front door. On one side of the yard was a huge tree throwing so much shade that the grass didn't grow there. A cement path led to a space on the side of the house with worn red bricks laid out in a random pattern, green moss and weeds peeping out between them. A thin trickle of water flowed out of the hill into a pool formed by rocks. The house itself was backed into the hill as if leaning on it for protection. The branches of the tree cuddled it, weaving its leaves onto the roof and windows.

Inside, the back rooms were dark, the only light came from the windows in the front. The first floor had no back windows and the second floor windows were about three inches from the side of the hill. The aura began to become more like Wuthering Heights, still romantic but very dark.

I went outside and sat on the top step, looking at the tree, dreaming about sitting there wearing a full skirted green gown, a huge picture hat shading my eyes, while boys gathered around to talk to such a gorgeous creature as me. I was fluttering my eyes at one of them when Mary's voice intruded: "What do you think?" she asked.

"He's so cute." I blushed as Mary gave me that 'you're daydreaming again' look.

Mama spoke at the same time: "Does it matter?" she said. "It's even darker than our house."

"Yes," said Mary, "that hill right up against it in back makes it feel kind of spooky. But the big windows in front help."

"Hhhmnnf!" was Mama's response.

"And there are enough bedrooms."

"It's a long hill to walk every day to the street car for me to go to work," Mama said. She had finally found a regular job, cooking at a restaurant on Forbes Street. "It's not a clean place," she had said, "but it's a job."

"Margie and Joe won't have to change schools. We're still in Annunciation Parish."

"Well, I guess we have to live someplace," Mama said. "It doesn't look any worse that the one we're in."

"Look, Mama," I called. "Look at the spring here. Those rocks must have been a spring house." I was thinking about Daddy. He would like that, he often talked about springs when he told stories about Ireland.

Mama leaned over the little pool of clear water and put her fingers under the tiny stream flowing over the rocks. Maybe she was remembering Ireland, too. "It's cold," she said, and abruptly shook the water off . "We'll have lots of cleaning to do here."

The owner accepted what we had for the house. Mama was still doubtful about it, but with no alternative, we bought it.

During the next two weeks, at Mama's insistence, we cleaned the Charles Street house. "I thought we were going to clean the new house, not this one," I said. "Why should we do this one when they're throwing us out anyhow?"

"Complain all you want," Mama said. "We're not leaving this house like a pig pen."

After we got all the rugs up, read all the old newspapers that were under them, piled clothes on furniture, and wrapped everything else in newspaper, Jackie got a truck and some help from a friend at work to do the moving. "Where's Daddy?" he asked once. Getting no answer from anybody and an Irish swear word from Mama, he grumbled: "He'll show up when all the work's done."

"If he does he'll have to look for us," Mama said.

We moved into the new house on Belleau Street. Three weeks went by and Daddy had still not come home, but Mama didn't seem to be worried. In fact, she was nicer to us, and didn't seem as tired as she used to be. I thought about Daddy, too. Maybe Jackie was right. The work was pretty much finished. Would Daddy be home soon?

The house was not as nice as our old one but I loved the tree and the spring. Sometimes I felt strange, though, almost sick at my stomach, the way I used to feel when I had to stay at my aunt's house for a week when I was in second grade. When I woke up at night in our Charles Street house I would listen for the sound of the street car as it went up the middle of the street. It was so close to the house that you could look down at the top of it from the third floor bedroom where Mary, Betty, Margie and I slept. Then I would think about the other outside noises: kids yelling "tin can alley!" long after we were in bed; neighbors sitting on their front steps, the sound of their voices encircling me with a nice cozy feeling.

The noises in the new house were from inside the house, not outside, and I was still trying to sort them out. The steps groaned under some mysterious pressure. There was a small metallic sound like the jaws of metal closing that came up through the heat vents in the furnace room. The leaves brushed against the window glass, sometimes with a sigh, other times with an angry swipe that hit with the force of driving rain. And there was the ghost.

Mama became tired and irritable, more so than she had been since the move. She said that she couldn't sleep all week. This was not anything new with Mama, she was always tired and we were used to it. I wondered if she missed Daddy, or if the strange house kept her awake. She finally asked Mary if she ever heard any strange noises but Mary said no. I had, but I was afraid to say anything thinking that Mama would simply say "Ora Musha, ye're always hearing things."

Mama took the smallest of the four bedrooms on the second floor. Her brass bed was against one wall, taking up most of the space. The brilliant colors - red, green and gold - in a picture of the Mother of Perpetual Help shone down from the wall facing the bed, and a small table stood near it. Mama's prayer book was usually beside the day's comic section of the paper, folded so that her 'story' was showing.

One night soon after we moved there, we heard a crash from her room and Mama yelling: "I'd throw it back at you if I could see you!" Mary and I ran down the hall and opened her bedroom door. She was sitting on the edge of the bed, her hair like a halo crown around her head. Mama always took her hair net off when she went to bed and her hair stuck out away from her neck, startled to be free. She was shaking her fist at the wall saying "I'll pray for your soul to be allowed into heaven and that's all you're going to get!" and didn't even notice us looking at her, so we went back to bed without asking what happened.

When I came downstairs the next morning, Mama was sitting at the dining room table, drinking tea and looking like she used to before we moved; forehead wrinkled in a frown, mouth turned down, fingers restlessly moving a salt shaker from one side of the table to the other. She was talking to herself.

"Well," she said in a whisper, "he's gone." Her hands became still. She looked across the table at the side window. Hiding behind the corner, I strained to look out the window without her seeing me, but there was nobody there. Her face changed, became quiet, like when she was telling her troubles to the Mother of Perpetual Help. I moved forward a little and my feet made a shuffling sound.

"Ora Musha, Anna, I might have known it was you." She was still looking toward the window.

"Who's gone?" I asked.

"Where are the others?" She looked beyond me. "Here's Mary. Are the others sleeping?"

"Yes," Mary said, giving a doubtful glance at me.

Mama gave a deep sigh. "Mr. Dorrington," she said. "Mr. Dorrington is gone."

We waited for her to say more but I could tell by her sidelong look that she was trying to decide whether to do so or not.

"Please, Mama," I said. What happened?"

"Well, now we know why we got the house so cheap," she said when she saw Mary and I staring at her. "Ah, well, Mr. Dorrington, the poor wandering soul. Maybe he will leave us alone now."

"Was that really Mr. Dorrington?" I asked. The story that one of the neighbors told her was that Mr. Dorrington had fallen down the steps from the second floor and died. He lived alone in the house and his body wasn't found for several days. The house had been rented before but nobody would stay in it. It was haunted, they said.

"Sure and it was himself," she said. "And who else would

be wandering around in the middle of the night? "

"The gall of him, throwing the clock across the room! Just to get my attention! He's been whispering and walking around and I let him go before. I said the prayers but he wouldn't leave. I'll say no more, but the devil's tricks are not going to make us leave this house. I thought all them ghosts were still in Ireland and here they are to bother me again."

"Again?" Mary and I said at the same time.

"You can ask your father about the boys who drowned in the ocean after drinking the poteen and kept the island haunted." she said.

Her voice dropped to a whisper. "Ah, Johnny," she said, her hand caressing the teapot, a small smile on her lips. "maybe he is just like you." She must have forgotten for a minute that we were there. How did she connect Mr. Dorrington with Daddy? I wondered if she missed Daddy sometimes when she wasn't mad at him and he was gone for a while and if he used to admire her and sing Irish songs to her the way he sometimes sang to us. "Ah now, you are either an angel or a devil. And how am I to know?" She took her hand off the teapot and pushed it aside. "God rest his soul" she murmured as she got up. Mary and I didn't know whether she was talking about Daddy or Mr. Dorrington.

The house was beginning to look nice. The front porch had been swept clean; most of the windows had lost their grimy overlay and now the sun glanced inside; the rocks around the little pool of water were orderly, forming a low wall. I was sitting on the wall, feeling the warm breeze, watching the wind toss the leaves of the tree when I saw Daddy. He was hunched forward, his legs stretching to conquer that last hill up to the house.

I remembered the first time I had seen him walking like that. When Joe was about three he had wandered away when Daddy was supposed to be watching him. Daddy was striding up a hill then, not one as steep as this one though, with close packed houses on each side of the canyon that he was hurrying through. For a few minutes then I was scared that Joe was really lost and Daddy would never find him. Then he appeared from around the corner with Joe in his arms. Daddy said he had been sitting on a curb in the next block, playing with a stick, poking at the dirt in the gutter. Daddy had scooped him up in his giant hands and was back down the hill in a minute. He didn't say a word but I thought he had been scared, too, from the way he held his head down and the jerky movements of his arms, swinging out from back to front like the giant pins connected to the locomotive wheels when it was rushing down the track.

Now he was wearing his old plaid flannel shirt and the same black pants that he always wore. He wears the same clothes winter and summer, I thought. Doesn't he ever get tired of those pants and that brown suit jacket, not part of a suit, just a jacket. When he saw me he stopped and took his cap off. "Ah, and this is where you are, is it?" he said and came over to where I was sitting.

"And what's this we have here? A spring, I see." He held his jacket and cap in his hand. I didn't say anything, just moved a little on the wall and he sat down beside me. His face looked like some of the cartoons of soldiers I had seen in the paper: bushy eyebrows, shaggy beard, hair hanging down over his ears. Even his eyes seemed to have some of that sad look that the soldiers had when they were joking about the war. Maybe he was scared, too.

"Yes," I said. I couldn't think of anything else to say to him. Any talking I had ever done had been in response to something: to Mama's demands that I ask him something; to calling him to come for a meal; to an "I don't know" in answer to funny questions like: "Who are you today? Anna Held or Clara Bow?" Most of the time I just listened to him talking under his breath as he was reading or humming some Irish tune or singing in the Irish when he was getting over being drunk.

"Ah, well," he said, and settled down on the little wall to contemplate the water.

I always associated the Belleau Street house with

Daddy, even though he didn't come to live there till after Mama got rid of the ghost. When he was there in cold weather, he spent his days in the living room, the only room with an open fireplace. He didn't like to make a fire and would get anybody who invaded his space to do it for him. I never minded, I liked the fire, too, so I came in and made it whenever I was home in the winter. He sat in the big overstuffed chair close to the fire, wearing the red checked flannel shirt, left leg crossed over the right, and watching me getting the fire started.

That summer he spent a lot of time on the front porch in an old rocking chair. He rebuilt the wall around the little pool and often brought a kitchen chair and sat by the spring in the shade from the overhanging trees. Sometimes when I was home, I sat on the wall near him and watched the drops of water making circles in the pool. I suspect that he was happier there than at any time since he left Ireland. He always had something to read, the newspaper or often books from a set of encyclopedias Mary had bought second hand. He talked Irish to himself, made notes on the pages of the book, and sang old Gaelic tunes, quietly, just loud enough for me to hear.

But I think it was the Charles Street house that held Mama's heart. It was the home that she loved; the one that she worked and fought so hard for. I think she missed the camaraderie with some of the neighbors and the ice man and the milk man; the warmth and companionship of the big light kitchen.

But she never went back, and I never went back there, either. What I left was not there anymore.

About the Author

Anna Strosser is the third of six children and the second of four daughters of Bridget McDonough and John Berry. After graduating from high school in Pittsburgh, she earned an R.N. in nursing. She went to college during her late forties to study art and was awarded a master's degree in art therapy when she was fifty seven years old.

Anna is married and has four children. She presently is retired from her work as an art therapist and lives in Philadelphia with her husband of fifty eight years, her daughter and son-in-law. She is now working on her next book about professional caretaking, healing herself and helping others to heal.

Breinigsville, PA USA
09 April 2010
235804BV00001B/48/P